Economics of Taxation

Economics of Taxation

Sayed Afzal Peerzade

ATLANTIC

PUBLISHERS & DISTRIBUTORS (P) LTD

Published by

ATLANTIC

PUBLISHERS & DISTRIBUTORS (P) LTD

7/22, Ansari Road, Darya Ganj, New Delhi-110002
Phones : +91-11-40775252, 40775214, 23273880, 23275880
Fax: +91-11-23285873
Web: www.atlanticbooks.com
E-mail: orders@atlanticbooks.com

Printed & bound in India by Atlantic Print Services

This humble work
is
dedicated to
my late teachers and mentors
Professor A.M. Khusro
Chairman, 11th Finance Commission
and
Dr. Muhammad Abbas Adhoni

Preface

In the study of public finance, taxation constitutes an important component and is being taught to the students of economics, business management and public administration in all colleges and universities. This volume is the outcome of lectures which I used to deliver to the students of Economics and Public Administration. It is comprised of 12 chapters dealing with different aspects of taxation.

In a world characterized by "asymmetric information" and "economic uncertainties", taxation is regarded as one of the three "glorious certainties". The other two are 'price rise' and 'death' which occur unannounced. Right from the emergence of state, the issue of taxation, for various reasons, has attracted great attention of governments, advisors to the governments and commoners. Governments' interest may be attributed to a desire to collect more revenue. Advisors are interested in the study of economic gains and efficiency losses that are so commonly associated with taxation. The commoners look at the whole process of taxation, sometimes with awe, anger and distrust and at other times, as a civilized method of discharging their duties as law-abiding honest citizens.

A special feature of the book is that some of the issues which normally receive a passing mention are discussed in detail. Another important feature is the non-mathematical treatment of some of the highly technical issues involved in taxation. Suitable figures, flow charts and tables are used extensively to make the subject matter more intelligible.

During the preparation of this book, I have, to a great extent, borrowed from "masters" and their "masterpieces". It is difficult to mention a few and leave others. I thank them all profusely. I express a deep sense of gratitude to my students and colleagues who, at different stages, discussed with me on a number of issues, and such discussions have been included in this volume. Thanks are also due to Atlantic Publishers and Distributors (P) Ltd., for evincing keen interest in the publication of this book.

The book will be extremely useful to the students of public finance, economics, public administration, business management and accounts and researchers in these fields. It shall be equally helpful to policymakers and advisors to the government and commoners in understanding the logic, utility and importance of taxation.

Sayed Afzal Peerzade

Contents

List of Tables and Charts

List of Figures

Taxation: Past, Present and Future

1

Objective: To examine changing perspective of the role of taxation in the context of dominant economic philosophies.

Organization: Changing perceptions; limited expenditure and taxation; major developments in early 20th century; market failures; the decades of 1950s and 1960s; broad dimensions of change; footsteps of Musgrave; decades of 1980s and 1990s; augmenting public finances; role of taxation; features and future prospects.

Changing Perceptions

The issue of taxation, both in the past and at present, may be analyzed by understanding and appreciating changing balance between three dominant economic philosophies which have greatly affected the role of government and thereby making of public policies. These are the libertarian, collectivist and neo-libertarian. The libertarians argue that private interests should take precedence over public interests and that the state has no right to redistribute incomes and wealth. Collectivists take a diametrically opposite stand rejecting supremacy of private interests. The neo-liberals take a stand which serves as a go-between the two.

The libertarian approach was developed in eighteenth and nineteenth centuries by Hume, Smith, Bentham and Mill. This is also regarded as classical liberal theory. The collectivist approach is normally associated with Karl Marx and his followers. Neo-liberal views were expounded in the twentieth century and are regarded as modern liberal theory. However, the range of views within the neo-liberals is very wide reflecting different interpretations of 'primacy of the individual', 'limited positive rights', 'enabling state', 'mixed economy', 'and modified markets'. "Put simply, the libertarian and collective political philosophies are much more absolutist and hence much clearer in terms of their beliefs than is the variable spectrum of neo-liberal philosophy." [1]

In the past, the classical economists, identified with the libertarian approach, assigned minimum role to the government.[2] The dominating philosophy was a firm belief in the efficacy of market mechanism. Adam Smith used the concept of invisible hand to explain the working of market forces. He was profoundly religious and saw the invisible hand as the mechanism by which the Benevolent God administered a universe in which human happiness was maximized. Adam Smith used the concept to describe the natural force that guides free market capitalism through competition for scarce resources. According to Adam Smith, in a free market, each participant tries to promote its self-interest. There is a contact amongst market participants, leading to an exchange of goods and services. The process of exchange enables each participant to be better-off than when simply producing for himself. He further said that in a free market, no regulation of any type is needed to ensure that the mutually beneficial exchange of goods and services continues. This invisible hand guides market participants to trade in the most mutually beneficial manner. It is, as Adam Smith points out, not from the benevolence of the butcher, the brewer, or the baker that we expect our dinner, but from their regard to their own interest. We address ourselves, not to their humanity but to their self-love.

---

1. Bailey, Stephen J., *Strategic Public Finance*, Palgrave, 2004, p. 7.
2. The names of Adam Smith, David Ricardo, R.T. Malthus and J.B. Say are normally included in the list of classical economists.

The notion of invisible hand is now popularly used to describe market forces. The classical economists believed that markets, in the absence of government control, have an inbuilt tendency to operate at an optimal level. It was argued that the very best of government is the one which governs least, spends less and imposes upon its people, least burden of taxation. They, therefore, thought that any intervention made by the government would amount to an unwanted and uncalled for intrusion disturbing efficient working of market forces.

What was then the role assigned by the classical economists to the government? They, under a strong influence of the efficacy of invisible hand, assigned a minimum role to the government. The role was restricted to the:

1. Maintenance of internal law and order thereby ensuring internal security.
2. Protection of lives and properties of people from foreign aggression by ensuring external security.
3. Erection and maintenance of certain public works such as roads, bridges, canals which contribute to the advancement of trade and commerce and educational institutions for the instruction of people.

In connection with the erection and maintenance of public works, Adam Smith remarks that "those public institutions and those public works which, though they may be in the highest degree advantageous to a great society, are, however, of such a nature that the profit could never repay the expense to any individual or small number of individuals, and which it, therefore, cannot be expected that any individual or small number of individuals should erect or maintain". J.S. Mill too was a believer in the philosophy of laissez faire. He remarks "Laissez faire should be the general practice: every departure from it, unless required by some great good, is a certain evil". Mill, however, favours a departure from laissez faire in respect of "ordinary" and "optional" functions. Ordinary functions of the state include defence and law and order. In addition to the ordinary functions, a government has to perform certain other functions for the convenience of people which include coinage, post and telegraph, setting of standard weights, road construction, street lighting, ports, lighthouses, etc. Mill gives the following reasons for state interference:

1. Individual may be unable to evaluate the utility of certain products, such as elementary education for children.
2. Lack of foresight may lead individuals to enter into irrevocable contracts from which they must be restrained.
3. In the case of delegation of powers by individuals to manager whose interests differ, state intervention may be needed. Regulation of monopolies is an example in this case. Mill's explanation why certain goods require public provision, thus, moved beyond Adam Smith's generalization but fell short of providing precise formulations.

Limited Expenditure and Taxation

The minimum role of government restricted the size of public spending on one hand and taxation on the other. It was not supposed that government would play an important role in the development of the country, provision of social security and construction and maintenance of infrastructure. Neither people demanded much from the government nor were there different platforms available to people to express their ideas and put forth their demands.[3]

Classical economists did not foresee benefits flowing from public expenditure and, therefore, they advocated minimum possible imposition of different taxes. Their notions of public expenditure and taxation were at the best, very narrow. A cursory look at their literature would enable us to have a broad understanding of the then stream of thought. Ricardo declared that if one wanted to have a peaceful government, one must reduce the size of budget. Ricardo "evidently found public expenditures so wasteful that he did not feel it necessary to discuss them. He was satisfied to endorse the golden maxim of Say that the very best of all plans is to spend little".[4] He also

3. Availability of different platforms is an interesting area of study in the public choice theory.
4. Musgrave Richard A., *The Theory of Public Finance: A Study in Public Economy*, McGraw-Hill Book Company, Inc., Tokyo, 1959, p. 68.

fell in line with J.B. Say who opined that the very best of all taxes was the one least in amount. Bastiat was more explicit; for him, the government cannot have any other rational function but the defence of individual rights. He went on to say that beyond justice, any intervention made by the government is an injustice. Henry Parnell stated that every particle of expenditure that is incurred beyond what necessity absolutely requires for preservation of social order and for protection against foreign attacks is waste and an unjust and oppressive imposition upon public. Gladstone is reported to have commented that it is better to leave money to fructify in the pockets of people instead of being taken away by taxation to be employed unproductively and even wastefully. Mill and his contemporaries regarded, under the above-mentioned background, progressive tax as a graduated form of robbery. The state was advised to keep its activities to a minimum level. It was believed that money spent privately did more good than public spending. In private sector, it was believed, money was more efficiently managed.

Major Developments in Early 20th Century

The passive role of the government continued till the early twentieth century. However, three important and consecutive developments shook the governments all over the world, more particularly in the West. These developments were:

1. Russian Revolution of 1917.
2. The Great Depression of 1930.
3. The publication of John Maynard Keynes' *General Theory* in 1936.

The greatest political and ideological development in the early 1920's was the Russian Revolution of 1917. It centered around a different economic ideology popularized by Karl Marx and practically implemented by Lenin and his comrades. The Marxian ideology was diametrically opposed capitalism and it offered an alternative system of economic and political governance. It had a great appeal to the labour class and its major plank was exploitation and subjugation of the labour class by the capitalists. Moreover, another shock was waiting for them in early 1930's when the Great Depression shook

American economy down under. During the time of crisis, the policy of *laissez faire* did not deliver desired results and the invisible hand got paralyzed, at least temporarily.

The Great Depression changed the contours of capitalism in three ways:

1. There was a clear recognition of role of the state in economic activities.
2. It was felt necessary that the state should provide safety nets to the most vulnerable sections of society.
3. Financial market should be brought under close supervision.

The publication of J.M. Keynes' *General Theory* further highlighted inherent weaknesses in the policy of *laissez faire.* Before Keynes, most economists and policy-makers accepted the highs and lows of business cycles as being as inevitable as the tides. The Keynesian attack also led to the destruction of one of the principles of sound finance, namely, the principle of balanced budget. Another principle of sound finance, namely, minimum expenditure became irrelevant. It suffices here to say that three major shocks changed the perception of the 3Ps [people, politicians and policy-makers] towards the role of government. The Russian Revolution generated political shock; the Great Depression provided economic shock and Keynes' *General Theory* created shock at the academic level.

Market Failures

In the context of above happenings, three major failures of market mechanism were identified as under:

1. Markets fail to regulate themselves and they are not in a position to avoid severe crisis such as Great Depression.
2. Markets do not efficiently address to the problem of unequal income, consumption and wealth distribution.
3. Markets are unable to provide public goods whose provision is desired on social and economic grounds.

In the backdrop of above mentioned developments, people in general and economists in particular started appealing for a more active role for the government. It is worth quoting Keynes here. In his toast to the Royal Economic Society in 1945, he said: "To economics and economists who are trustees not of civilization but of the possibilities of civilization." In the place of classical dictum of "supply creates its own demand", Keynes established a new proposition that "demand creates its matching supply".

The governments in different countries were asked upon to generate employment, provide social security and facilitate economic development. The argument was developed on the lines that markets were not in general efficient; that there was an important role for government to play; Adam Smith's invisible hand is invisible, at least in part, because it is not there.

The Decades of 1950s and 1960s

In the early 1950s and 1960s, a number of countries in Asia and Africa secured independence from centuries of colonial rules. These countries were in a great hurry to make for the lost time and resources. Consequently, their governments had to shoulder great responsibilities in facilitating and financing economic development. Thus, the scope of government intervention started expanding beyond the traditional functions, i.e., maintenance of internal law and order and protection of boundaries from foreign aggression. Governments were asked to assume such responsibilities which markets had so far avoided.[5]

Footsteps of Musgrave

Now, following the footsteps of Musgrave[6] and Bailey[7], the economic functions of government are classified into four main categories:

---

5. In recent years, a new branch of economics popularly known as public sector economics has emerged which studies, in particular, the role of government from different angles.
6. Musgrave, Richard A., *The Theory of Public Finance*, McGraw-Hill, 1959, pp. 5-27.
7. Bailey, Stephen J., *Public Sector Economics: Theory Policy and Practice*, Palgrave, 2002, pp. 17-47.

1. To overcome inefficiencies in the market in allocation of resources [allocative role].
2. To redistribute income, wealth and consumption in manner considered to be just and fair [redistributive role].
3. To control and regulate cyclical movements [stabilizing role].
4. To legislate and enforce laws of contract, consumer protection, justice and so on, in order that the market economy may function [regulatory role].

The government pursues a scheme of allocation of resources that maximizes economic welfare. This is generally referred to as allocative efficiency or the 'first best' allocation of resources. The government has to deal with the market distortions caused by monopoly power and other forms of market failure. In its distributive role, the government balances allocative efficiency with equity in the allocation of resources by using taxation, social security and the distribution of public sector services to influence the distribution of income. Similarly, fiscal instruments are fine-tuned to avoid cyclical fluctuations. Sometimes, these are expansionary and at others, contractionary in nature. While the allocative, distributive and regulatory roles are microeconomic in nature, the stabilization role is macroeconomic in nature using fiscal, monetary and other economic policies to pursue the objectives of control of inflation, unemployment and so on.

Joseph Stiglitz is of the view that the role of government can be viewed as establishing infrastructure in its broadest sense—the educational, technological, financial, physical, environmental and social infrastructure of the economy.[8] Since markets cannot operate in a vacuum, this infrastructure is necessary if markets are to fulfill their central role in increasing wealth and living standards. Because constructing the broad infrastructure is beyond the capacity or interest of any single firm, it must be primarily the responsibility of government. In

---

8. Stiglitz, Joseph E., "The Role of Government in Economic Development" in A. Bagchi (ed.) *Readings in Public Finance*, Oxford University Press, New Delhi, 2005, pp. 159-62.

this context, Stiglitz envisions six important universal roles for governments:

1. Promoting Education.
2. Promoting Technology.
3. Supporting the Financial Sector.
4. Investing in Infrastructure.
5. Preventing Environmental Degradation.
6. Creating and Maintaining a Social Safety Net.

Stiglitz assigns a special role to governments in developing and transition economies.[9] In such economies, markets are either lacking or the ones that do exist may function less effectively, and information problems are more severe than in industrial countries simply because of the rapid change in the economic environment. While market failures loom larger in developing and transition economies, the capacity of the government to correct these market failures is often weaker. Assessing the appropriate role of government requires recognition of both the need for and the limitations of government action. Successful governments have helped create markets. Governments and markets are, thus, not competitive but complementary to each other.

Broad Dimensions of Change

Thus, we can notice a considerable change in the perspective of people in general and economists and policy-makers in particular towards the role of government. Broad dimensions of the change are as under:

1. Governments are now more active than before; they are not mute spectators of social and economic commotion.
2. The size of public expenditure has increased and governments are now spending more than before. Deficit financing is a common feature.
3. Governments are now taxing more than before. There are now more taxes, more people and transactions are taxed and these are collected at high rates.

Each of the above mentioned areas of government intervention and the means of intervention are debatable.

9. *Ibid.*

Universally, however, fiscal inaction of governments is highly undesirable. Governments are expected to combat unemployment and bring stability in the economy through suitable changes in the levels of taxation and public expenditure. How, in its most elementary form, the fiscal policy functions, is explained in the following Fig. 1.1.

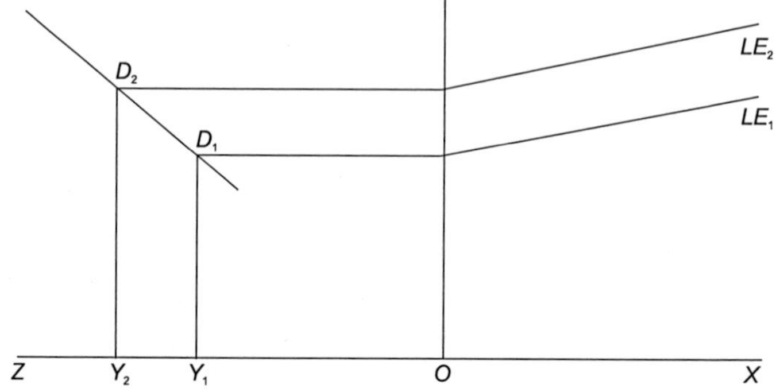

Fig. 1.1: Fine Tuning of Fiscal Policy

Let us assume that the inadequate demand calling forth current output has brought down the level of employment and output from LE_0 (not in Fig. 1.1) to LE_1. This employment level is supported by D_1 of demand, which is generated by Y_1 level of disposable income. At this juncture, to avoid a further fall in the level of employment, the government follows an expansionary fiscal policy, which injects new purchasing power into the economy to the extent of Y_1Y_2. This generates D_2 of demand, which in turn pushes the level of employment from LE_1 to LE_2. Thus, the fine-tuning of fiscal policy as suggested by economists from time to time goes a long way in raising the levels of output and employment and preventing economy from falling into deep depression. Keynes was, therefore, perfectly right in regarding economists as trustees of civilization. Every moment of mismanagement diminishes the chances of survival. Since that historic toast of 1945, the scope of government activities has been gradually widening and today budget is considered as an instrument to influence the working of economy, *a la* Plowden.

The Decades of 1980s and 1990s

Keynesian economic policies seem to have worked from the late 1940s through to the early 1970s. It, however, became increasingly difficult for governments to raise required revenue to finance their ever-expanding roles. The levels of public expenditures, public borrowing, public debt and taxation, rose phenomenally. Despite this in many developed countries, the rapid growth rates of 1950s-1970s could not be sustained. "The general acceptance of the all-powerful state and its ability to solve economic and social problems began to break down."[10] This led to a change in perception towards the role of state. Arguments were developed to highlight that states were growing out of control, increasingly seeking to control the lives of their citizens and stifling economic prosperity by regulating market forces and higher doses of taxation. Efficiency costs were claimed to higher than the gains from taxation notwithstanding the rent-seeking activities. "Thus, neo-liberals such as Hayek and Friedman argue that cradle-to-grave welfare states are counterproductive in making economies less productive by crowding out the private sector: public finance *crowds out* private finance."[11]

The neo-liberal approach led to the emergence of what is now popularly known as "supply side economics". Its arguments were widely accepted within developed countries during 1980s and 1990s and had profound impact on developing economies. At this juncture, one should note the content of a change in Indian economic policy too. Since the dawn of planning era, it was facilitating a license, permit and quota *raj*. In 1980s and 1990s, it gave into liberalization, privatization and globalization heralding an era of New Economic Policy.[12] "Whilst the libertarian and collectivist schools have been very influential at a philosophical level, it is

10. Bailey, Stephen J., *op. cit.*, p. 13.
11. *Ibid.*
12. This is not to say that there are no critics of NEP. Its failure in the areas of employment generation and income redistribution are well documented.

the neo-liberal school that has been most influential for public policy."[13]

Augmenting Public Finances

With due respect to the changing balance between the dominant economic philosophies, it is maintained here that the efficacy of government intervention into different areas of economic polity depends greatly upon its ability to raise resources. These can be raised internally and externally and through tax and non-tax means. It is, however, better in broad national interest that a maximum emphasis should be placed on a greater possible exploitation of internal resources. The broad ways of augmenting public finances internally are listed in the following Table 1.1[14]:

Table 1.1: Sources of Public Finance

Sl. No.	Sources	Examples
1.	Taxes	Personal income taxes; expenditure taxes; corporate income tax; capital gains tax; inherited wealth taxes; property taxes; land taxes; payroll taxes; per capita taxes [lump-sum poll taxes]; environmental taxes; other taxes
2.	Charges	User-charges; rents; processing/administration fees.
3.	Privatization/sales	Land, buildings, enterprise, equipments, cultural artifacts; leases and so on
4.	Borrowing	Domestic and foreign sources
5.	State Lotteries	Central; regional; local levels
6.	Donations/bequests	In the form of cash and/or physical assets
7.	Payments in kind	In the form of physical assets instead of user-charges
8.	Special assessments	Voluntary payment of extra taxes for specific improvements to property

13. Bailey, Stephen J., *op. cit.*, p. 14.
14. Bailey, Stephen J., *Strategic Public Finance*, Palgrave, 2004, p. 132.

In any case, the above-enumerated sources are not exhaustive and complete. We may add some other sources such as surcharge, entertainment taxes, entry taxes, gift taxes, service taxes, interest receipts and recovery of loans, etc.

Role of Taxation

There is a near consensus among economists that of the above-mentioned means, taxation should be used with utmost care. It is held that the way to economic development is not the easy path of lower taxation and minimum government activity. The success of economic policies greatly depends upon, first, mobilizing resources through taxation and secondly, efficiently transferring the resources for public purposes. The size of public expenditure and thereby government intervention depends greatly upon resource mobilization on one hand and transfer of resources from private to public uses on the other. It is in this context that different types of taxes on persons, commodities, services and transactions fit eminently into government schema. These may be introduced using proportional and progressive rates.

Observable limits to taxation are very clear in both the introduction and administration of different taxes. Designing rate structure is also an uphill task. Nonetheless, for a variety of reasons, governments are placing a heavy trust on personal and commodity taxes as there is an observed interrelationship between taxation and public expenditure decisions. In sharp contrast to the older notions, taxation today is considered as a means of transferring scarce resources from private to public use for what is often described as more judicious and productive spending; correcting personal and regional disparities; regulating markets and controlling cyclical fluctuations. It is observed that the extent to which accretion to national income following economic development can get siphoned off into the national exchequer by taxation becomes a crucial factor in the process of economic development.

Taxation has an important role to play in developing countries too. Here, economic and financial compulsions are greatly different from those in developed countries. Within the group of developing countries, there are some which are growing very fast and others struggling to grow. In this context, the role of taxation is envisioned as under:

1. It should mobilize and channel economic surplus into productive channels.
2. It should provide sufficient incentives to save and invest.
3. It should curb wasteful consumption expenditure.
4. It should efficiently transfer resources from private to public use for spending on socially desirable projects.
5. It should modify the pattern of investment in line with the broad objectives of economic policy.
6. It should aim at curbing income, consumption and wealth inequalities.

Thus, from a dependable means of revenue to the national exchequer, taxation has now come to play a multidimensional role. Over the years, its importance as a fiscal tool has increased considerably. Developing as well as developed countries are using different taxes to achieve more than one goal of economic policy. Every aspect of taxation is strongly debated and the debate goes on.

Features of a Good Tax System

In the context of U.S. tax system, Musgrave remarks that the U.S. tax system, like that of any other country, has developed in response to many influences: economic, political and social. It has not been constructed by a master architect in line with the optimal requirements for a good tax structure.[15] Yet, economists and social philosophers, right from Adam Smith, have propounded what such requirements should be. What is true in case of U.S. is also true in case of other countries of the world. In several countries, taxes were introduced as temporary measures but later on, became a permanent feature.

---

15. Musgrave, Richard A. and Peggy B. Musgrave, *Public Finance in Theory and Practice,* Fifth Edition, Tata McGraw-Hill, 2004, Chapters 18, 19 and 20.

Normally, "goodness" of tax system is defined and explained with a reference to the four famous canons of taxation as developed by Adam Smith. These are: (1) Canon of Equality, (2) Canon of Economy, (3) Canon of Certainty and (4) Canon of Simplicity. Later on, two more canons were added namely, canon of productivity and canon of elasticity. "More generally", writes Bailey, "a strategically optimal tax system is one that as far as possible promotes the achievement of the 4Es:"[16] Equity; Efficiency; Economy and Effectiveness.

The sum and substance of all the above-mentioned canons, reflecting the essence of a good tax system, is outlined as under:

1. Revenue yield should be adequate.
2. The distribution of tax burden should be equitable. Everyone should be made to pay his or her fair share.
3. Taxes should be chosen to minimize interference with economic decisions in otherwise efficient markets. Excess burden should be minimized.
4. Tax structure should facilitate the use of fiscal policy for stabilization and growth objectives.
5. Tax system should permit fair and non-arbitrary administration and should be understandable to the taxpayer.
6. Administrative and compliance cost should be as low as is compatible with other objectives.

What Future Holds for Taxation?

In coming years, on account of privatization, liberalization and globalization, countries all over the world will be highly sensitive to their own tax policies and also tax policies pursued in other countries. These policies are likely to affect competitive edge of one country over the other universally. At the level of personal taxation, more concern will be shown

16. Bailey, Stephen J., *op. cit.*, p. 136.

towards efficiency loss. The taxation scenario may be expected to be as under:

1. As personal incomes are growing fast, the personal income tax will continue to remain a major direct tax.
2. In the area of personal taxation, the dominant philosophy will be making the tax bases as broad as possible.
3. Emphasis will be on administering low tax rates.
4. There will be minimum but broad slabs and thereby fewer rate bands.
5. Taxation of fringe benefits at company will continue.
6. New forms of wealth will emerge and these need to be taxed.
7. VAT or GST [goods and services tax] will operate throughout the country with one or two rates. Both or either of these two taxes will be an important source of revenue because the service sector, *vis-à-vis* agriculture and industry, is growing at a phenomenal rate.

Approach to Taxation

2

Objective: To examine different approaches to taxation and study their different manifestations.

Organization: The Benefit Approach; two Interpretations of benefit approach; genesis of Benefit Approach; convergence of two Approaches; assessment of Benefit Principle; ability to Pay Approach; assessment of Ability to Pay; different indices; equity and rate structure.

Once it is realised that the payment of taxes is unavoidable, at different levels and by all the sections of the population either directly or indirectly, the next issue to examine is the approach towards taxation. Musgrave is of the view that: "Views on the principles of taxation may be found in the writings of innumerable authors, philosophers, economists and political theorists from middle ages to date; and this is for good reason: The duty to pay taxes or the power to tax is among the most tangible of all links between subject and sovereign or citizen and society."[1] The question now is not why the taxes should be paid but what should be the approach. Traditionally, economists and fiscal theorists have confined themselves to two approaches namely:

1. The Benefit Approach or Principle
2. The Ability to Pay Approach or Principle.

---

1. Musgrave, Richard A., *The Theory of Public Finance: A Study in Public Economy,* McGraw-Hill Book Company Inc., Tokyo, 1959, p. 61.

These two approaches are examined as under which have something to contribute and both have certain serious limitations.

The Benefit Approach or Principle

Traditionally, the benefit approach has provided a justification for the imposition of different types of taxes. Initially, it was thought that since all lands belong to the king or queen, their subjects should pay some amount of money. Later, the kings or queens started laying their hands on the produce of the land. Thus, the land was taxed twice, first the land itself was the base and secondly, the produce from same land was taxed. The argument here was very simple. Since the lands belong to the kings and queens, their subjects are, thus, benefited from royal possessions. This was the earliest explanation of the notion of benefit.

As the time passed, the concept of benefit was widened to cover other benefits received by people from the government expenditures funded by taxation. In this context, it is worth to recall the classical perception that three distinct benefits accrue to people:

(1) Benefits from the protection of lives and properties of people by the state.

(2) Benefits from the protection when borders are protected from foreign aggression.

(3) Benefits from certain works which the state erects and maintains in public interest.

Two Interpretations of the Benefit Approach

There are two interpretations of benefit approach. First, the cost of service principle and secondly, the value of service principle. The cost of service interpretation signifies that the beneficiaries should bear the cost of provision of the benefit. The beneficiaries should contribute by the way of different taxes to the expenditure incurred by the state. Here the entire approach gets personalised in the sense that the benefits received and amount to be paid in taxes are individualised.

Here, in the opinion of J.S. Mill, emphasis is placed on *quid pro quo* relation between the state and its people.

The value of service interpretation requires that every individual should contribute to the national exchequer according to the value of benefits received. This leads us to find out an appropriate measure of value and apportioning of contribution in relation to the benefits received. Should it be equal, more or less than the benefits received? Developing a measure of value is really a demanding task.

Genesis of Benefit Approach

During 17th and 18th centuries, the benefit principle came to be invariably associated with the contract theory of the state as popularised by Hobbes, Locke, Rousseau, Hume and German authors namely Grotius and Pufendorf and others. The basis of contract, as understood then, was the protection provided by the state. Protection, thus, became the reason for taxation and taxes came to be considered a natural price paid for receiving protection. It was argued that the lives and properties of people were normally insecure and, therefore, society must be formed to protect the two. Taxes were, thus, regarded "as membership fee for living in an organised society". Logically, the contract theory may be attributed to the then perception of limited role of government. Here, we can visualise two parties. The one is protector, i.e., the state and the other being the protectorates, i.e., the subjects of every state.

Writers such as McCulloch, Thiers, Mazzola, and de Viti de Marco contributed to the evolution of benefit principle. They argued that taxes were premium paid for protection and public services should be restricted to those who pay for it. De Viti de Marco maintains that there exists an exchange relationship between the state and its subjects. The argument runs as follows: "The duty of citizens to pay taxes was matched by the duty of the state to provide public services."

In the later part of 18th century with the publication of Adam Smith's *Wealth of Nations*, the classical economics made its appearance. The greatest-happiness principle as developed by Bentham and other utilitarian authors tried to replace the protection principle of contract theorists. These authors, however, were not fully successful in totally replacing the element of protection in the theory of contract which was considered necessary for happiness. Earlier writers who supported the benefit principle argued in terms of protection and concluded in favour of proportional taxation.

Convergence of the Two Approaches

We can notice the convergence of two approaches at the time of their evolution itself. Much before Adam Smith, William Petty argued: "It is generally allowed by all that men should contribute to the public charge but according to the share and interest, they have in the public peace; that is, according to their estates and riches". This statement of Petty has two components. First, "share and interest in public peace" and secondly, "estates and riches". "Share and interest in public peace" is a result of overall protection for which people should contribute to the exchequer. By and large, people are interested in "public peace" because it facilitates economic activities. Now they should bear the cost of maintaining "public peace" according to their respective "estates and riches".

A classical statement pertaining to the convergence is that of Adam Smith who writes: "The subjects of every state ought to contribute towards the support of government as nearly as possible in proportion to their respective abilities; that is, proportion to the revenue which they respectively enjoy under the protection of the state". The element of benefit principle is found in Adam Smith's mention of "revenue which people enjoy under the protection of the state". Protection as provided by the state ensures a steady flow of revenue to the protectorates. But, how are the benefits flowing from protection and resultant revenue are to be measured? Since there is no practical way of doing this, a general rule of thumb is needed in place of individual estimation of benefits. This rule, according to Adam Smith, is provided by taxing individuals "in proportion to their respective abilities", that is, the revenue which they respectively enjoy under the protection of the state. The element of ability to pay principle is visible in Adam Smith's mention of "in proportion to their respective abilities". According to Musgrave: "Smith, thus, shrewdly inserted an ability element into the weak link of the benefit rule."[2] Musgrave, however, claims that Adam Smith belongs to "the benefit camp".

An Assessment of Benefit Principle

The benefit principle has certain inherent advantages which are enumerated as under:

1. It establishes a clear reason for taxing people.
2. By harping upon the benefit component, the state may arouse emotional sentiments of people to pay taxes honestly and regularly.
3. It has a clear edge over the ability to pay approach wherever it is possible to impose users' charges. Here, "money follows the user". It would encourage service providers to respond more to citizens' preferences.

At the same time, the benefit principle suffers from the following shortcomings:

1. As the perception of people and policy-makers towards the role of government has changed in the recent times, the benefit principle as envisioned in its original form has lost its validity.[3]
2. We are yet to develop an objective criterion of measuring the benefits received from the state services such as defence, law and order, basic health and universal education and other facilities. It is easy to calculate expenses incurred, rupee by rupee, but is hopelessly difficult to measure benefits. It is a highly subjective matter.
3. A strict application of benefit principle leads to regressive taxation. It is wrong to maintain that benefits from defence and law and order accrue equally to all regardless of their economic status.

---

2. Musgrave, *op. cit.*, p. 67.
3. Readers are advised to refer to the first chapter of this book wherein the changing perception has been highlighted.

When examined closely, it is clear that people with "estates and riches" are more benefited than those who do not possess them. In times of war and internal disturbances, other than their lives, poor have nothing significant to lose whereas rich people have very high stakes. This approach is regressive, as it makes no difference between the rich and poor in the matters of benefits and apportioning of tax burden. Thus, when applied blindly, it leads to injustice rather than justice in the matters of taxation.

4. The instrument taxation as perceived under the benefit approach is not helpful as a redistributive and stabilising tool of overall economic policy. It places the state in a "semi-commercial" position.

In conclusion, it can be said that the shortcomings of benefit approach outnumber its advantages. The problem that "who benefits most from government expenditures funded by taxation" continues to haunt this approach. In several such cases, benefits remain untraced. It has limited uses. It may be applied in certain cases where it is easy to identify direct beneficiaries of certain services provided by the state.

The Ability to Pay Approach

The broad assumption of ability to pay principle is that those who are able to pay taxes should pay. On account of its underlying principle, the benefit approach has received popular support and acclaim. Its logical extension is that those who, because of their poverty and limited means are unable to pay, should not pay taxes. On the contrary, they are expected to receive financial support from the government. This has led to birth of an idea known as the *negative income taxation.*

In the discussion on the principles of taxation, the advocacy that the ability to pay approach should be applied has run parallel with the benefit principle. Musgrave claims that it even predates the benefit approach.[4] Its supporters have

4. Musgrave, *op. cit.*, p. 91.

a respectable ancestry. Guicciardini and Jean Bodin are regarded its precursors. Guicciardini, favouring the ability principle, argued for the progressive taxation. Bodin, subscribing to the ability principle, pleaded for proportional taxation. Rousseau, Sismondi, Say, Mill, Wagner, Roosevelt, etc., on one ground or the other, lent their support to the ability to pay principle.

The statement of J.S. Mill is considered as the classical version of ability to pay principle. Rejecting the popular notion of provision of protection as the basis of contract, Mill argued that insistence on the benefit principle could lead to regressive taxation as poor are more in need of protection. This insistence, he added, would be the reverse of true idea of justice. He opined that protection is not the *only function* of government but the functions of government go much beyond protection.

The ability to pay approach draws its support from the dictum that all should be treated equally under the law. "For what reason ought equality to be the rule in matters of taxation? For the reason that it ought to be so in all affairs of government". And so the argument continues, "equality in taxation means equality of sacrifice."[5] It means apportioning the contribution of each person towards the expenses of government so that he will be neither more nor less inconvenient from his share of payment than every other person experiences from his.

An Assessment of Ability to Pay Approach

In several respects, the ability to pay approach is superior to the benefit approach. On the face of it, the ability to pay principle successfully avoided the chances of regressive taxation. Further, it made it possible to divorce expenditure decisions from those of taxation. Regardless of the benefits accruing to different persons, each one should contribute to the national exchequer as nearly as possible in relation to one's ability.

---

5. Mill quoted by Musgrave, *op. cit.*, p. 92.

The ability to pay principle contains in itself a psychological component. Mill has raised the issue of "convenience/inconvenience" which is purely psychological. A taxpayer gets satisfaction that he is asked to pay according to his ability, neither more nor less. He also feels satisfied that others too, regardless of benefits received, are contributing their share to the national exchequer.

It is worth recalling here that in case of benefit approach, the ghost of measuring benefits haunted its supporters. There was no consensus among economists in respect of measurement of benefits. In the same fashion, it can be said that the ability to pay principle is marred by two very distinct difficulties. First, what are the manifestations of the ability to pay? Secondly, once known, how to measure them?

Manifestations of Ability to Pay: Different Indices

Generally speaking, there are three indices of ability to pay and these serve the purpose of basis for charge. These are income, wealth and consumption of a taxpayer. A person may be taxed at the one and same time for his income, wealth and consumption. Since time immemorial, wealth or property was considered as the best index of ability to pay. Accumulation of wealth was a matter of prime importance to individuals and nations as well. It is appropriately clear from the very title of the book penned by Adam Smith. He titled it as *The Wealth Nations*. In the Elizabethan poor law, the ability or faculty was expressed in terms of property. The same was the case in early legislation of American colonies.[6]

As the time passed by there took place three important revolutions first being industrial revolution followed by revolution in transportation and revolution in communication. These revolutions changed the nature of pecuniary economy and consequently, there took place a shift in emphasis on income rather than property as an index of ability to pay. Currently, it is held that property is not the main source of income though it continues to remain an important one. It may or may not yield income sufficient to a person to be qualified

6. Musgrave, *op. cit.*, p. 94.

as taxpayer. Any tax on property, in the absence of sufficient income from it, may gradually lead to its depletion. Presently, in almost all countries, taxes on property are considered as additional sources of revenue. These are supplemented with taxes on income and consumption.

Although even today wealth constitutes an important base, the income base has dislodged it from prime position it enjoyed in ancient times. Adam Smith formulated his first maxim in terms of income only. The tax based upon personal income has become a more popular form of direct taxation. Over the years, it has turned out to be a dependable means of revenue and a powerful tool in the fiscal armoury of the state to achieve certain desired goals of fiscal policy.

For the purpose of taxation, income from all sources is computed on accrual basis. Income tax is, however, imposed on income which is arrived at after allowing certain exemptions and deductions. Despite several inherent advantages, there is, however, a classical debate in economics literature over the appropriateness of income tax as an equitable tax.[7] Musgrave admits: "Even if an accretion concept of income is accepted as the proper index of ability to pay, it is far from clear how accretion should be defined in concrete cases. Along with the growth of modern economic society and its increasing complexities, these difficulties have grown by leaps and bounds".[8]

There is also a school of thought which suggests that the index of ability to pay should be defined as consumption rather than income. A direct tax based on consumption is known as an expenditure tax in India and United Kingdom. In United States of America, it is known as spendings tax.[9] It was

---

7. Problems associated with income base are discussed in detail in Chapter 5.
8. Musgrave, *op. cit.*, p. 94.
9. Relative merits and demerits of consumption based are discussed in detail in Chapter 6.

introduced for a brief period in India and Sri Lanka where it failed to take-off.[10]

Irving Fisher in United States and Nicholas Kaldor in United Kingdom were two of the most vocal supporters of consumption-based direct expenditure tax. Its theoretical superiority was recognised even by Keynes. We, however, note that no country has replaced its income tax by an expenditure tax. Direct taxes on wealth and consumption are administered but as supplemental levies.

Ability to Pay, Equity and Rate Structure

Ignoring the arguments, both for and against different indexes of ability to pay, let us stick to income as the basis for charge. Here the principle of equality requires that in the matters of taxation, all taxpayers should be treated equally. People with equal income should pay equal tax and *vice versa.* Two major questions arising here are: What is the precise meaning of term equal sacrifice in the context of equality? At what rate people should pay tax?

The issue of equal sacrifice is both one of the oldest and also one of the most important problems in public finance. In one way or the other, it remains to this day one of the unresolved issues in public finance. The issues raised are similar to the social welfare function. The essence of ability to pay approach is that taxpayers should make an equal sacrifice as and when they pay taxes. Since the times of John Stuart Mill, taxpayers are said to be treated equally if their tax payments involve an equal sacrifice or loss of welfare. The loss of welfare in turn is related to the loss of income as measured by the taxpayers' marginal utility of income schedule.[11] The issue that taxpayers should make sacrifice is clear. What less clear, however, is: what means equal sacrifice? Does it mean equal absolute loss of utility or equal proportional loss of utility or equal marginal loss of utility?

---

10. For further details, readers are advised to refer Sayed Afzal Peerzade's *Expenditure Tax in India: Feasibility, Problems and Prospects,* Anmol Publications, New Delhi, 1990.
11. Musgrave Richard and Pebby B. Musgrave, *Public Finance in Theory and Practice,* 5th Edition, Tata McGraw Hill, New Delhi, 2004, p. 228.

1. *Equal Absolute Sacrifice*

The meaning of equal absolute sacrifice is that the total loss of utility on account of imposition of tax should be equal for all taxpayers. Under this scheme of things, a taxpayer who has more income will pay more tax and the one has less will pay less tax but the sacrifice to both as a result of the tax should be equal. On account of its visible fairness, this principle has received popular support.

2. *Equal Proportional Sacrifice*

Here the loss of utility on account of imposition of a tax is proportional to the total income of taxpayers. Taxpayers with higher incomes pay more amount of money in tax than those with low incomes but in proportionate terms, the burden is same.

3. *Equal Marginal Sacrifice*

Here the marginal sacrifice on account of payment of taxes should be same. In case of taxpayers in high-income brackets, the marginal utility of money is low and it is high for taxpayers in low-income brackets. This implies that a taxpayer in high-income bracket should pay more tax as compared to the one in low-income bracket. There are, however, two major concerns. First, the shape of marginal utility schedule should be known. Secondly, the same schedule is applies to all taxpayers. Neither of these two conditions is met. In the opinion of Musgrave and Musgrave, the science of psychology does not provide answer to the first concern as above and that there is reason to believe that capacities to derive utility do in fact differ among individuals.[12]

Application of Tax Rates to Tax Base

It is possible that our choice of the "best tax base" gets vitiated by the application of improper rates to that base. Thus, the choice of rates is also as important as the choice of tax base itself. Here we shall classify rate schedules under three general categories namely proportion rates, progressive rates and regressive rates.

---

12. Musgrave and Musgrave, *op. cit.*, p. 231.

A schedule of proportional tax rates is one in which the rate of taxation remains constant as the tax base changes. A schedule of progressive tax rates is one in which the rate of taxation increases as the tax base increases. A schedule of regressive tax rates is one in which the rate of taxation decreases as the tax base increases. Thus, recognising that the amount of tax payable is the result of multiplying the base by the rate, in the case of a proportional tax the multiplier remains constant which changes in the multiplicand; in a progressive tax, the multiplier increases as the multiplicand increases; in a regressive tax, the multiplier decreases as the multiplicand increases. Diagrammatically, the differences are shown in three different panels of the following Fig. 2.1.

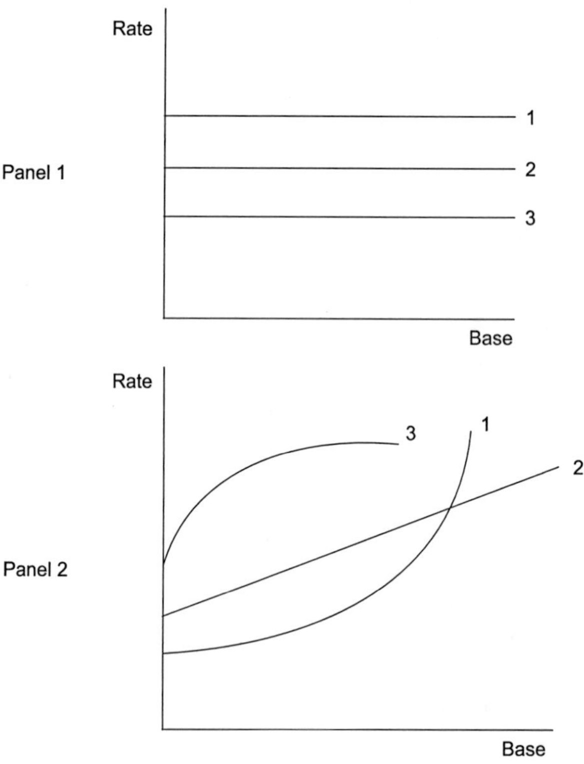

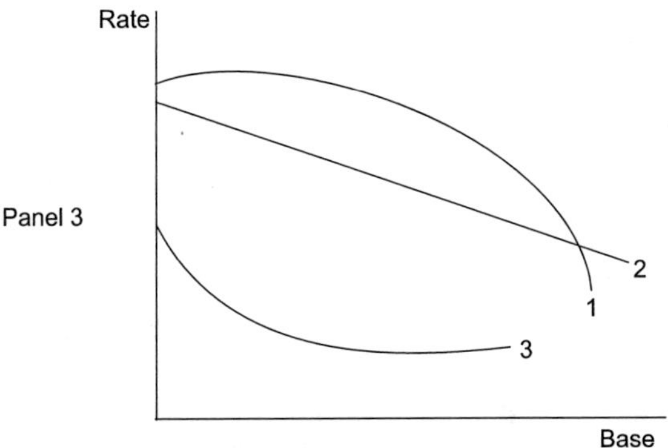

Fig. 2.1: Rate Schedules
Panel 1: Proportional Tax: Alternative Rate Schedules
Panel 2: Progressive Tax: Alternative Rate Schedules
Panel 3: Regressive Tax: Alternative Rate Schedules.

By definition, a proportional rate schedule can be established at any level, provided the rate remains constant at that level. A progressive rate schedule offers many slope patterns, all of which represent progression so long as any increase in the base is accompanied by an increase in the rate. The same is true of regression provided the rate decreases when the base increases. A tax rate schedule may combine more than one of the types shown. It is common for income tax rates to progress by brackets and within the brackets remain proportional.

Taxes all over the world are either proportional or progressive. For example, sales and excise taxes, taxes on employments and callings, property taxes, some business taxes, etc., are mainly proportional. Taxes on personal incomes and on some corporations are mainly progressive. There are no examples of regressive taxes. Their study, however, is significant at least in theory.

Progressive taxation is a fact of our time. The average person instinctively accepts the principle of progression as an article of faith and governments implement this principle in the formulation of rate schedules for important tax measures.[13]

13. Taylor, Philip E., *The Economics of Public Finance,* Third Edition, Oxford and IBH, 1965, p. 297.

Briefly speaking the case for progressive taxation rests on the following grounds:

1. Revenue productivity.
2. Optimum individual allocation of tax burden.
3. Promotion of stability and growth.
4. Optimum social allocation of resources.

While there is near consensus among economists on the suitability of progression, they greatly differ over the degree of progression. This issue has acquired significance in the context of "dead weight loss."[14] The popular argument is that a tax should involve minimum "dead weight loss" and it is minimum when tax rates are proportional and not progressive.

14. Discussed in detail separately in this book.

Issues in Taxation

3

Objective: To examine various issues related to taxation.

Organization: Test of suitability; equity; efficiency; simplicity; optimal administration; costs of taxation and tax expenditure.

Fiscal inaction and tax neutrality are things of past. Taxation today exerts a powerful impact on the level of economic activity. Decisions to work, save, invest, spend, bear risk are generally affected by changes in tax rates. A good tax system may be defined as one which yields required amount of revenue with no or minimum adverse effects. It ensures a best trade-off between equity and efficiency. In practice, if it is not possible to have a good tax system, at least, then, attempts should be made in the direction of one with a minimum possible drift away from the good.

The suitability of having a particular tax or a combination of different taxes is a very complicated question. It all depends upon, in addition to value judgments, short-run and long-run requirements of an economy. Sometimes, it is crucial, taking into account a set of objectives, either to introduce new taxes or to withdraw few taxes or to vigorously administer existing taxes. It is also necessary to revise regularly exemption limits, review the width of slabs, examine the height of different rates, examine nature and scope of allowable deductions, tax concessions, etc.

Test of Suitability

Economists have put forth the following test to examine the suitability of having a particular tax base. It is a test that revolves around:

1. Equity
2. Efficiency
3. Simplicity.

These issues are examined as under:

1. *Equity*

Equity is one of the classical canons taxation. It is fundamental to taxation having two distinct dimensions; horizontal equity and vertical equity. Horizontal equity requires equal treatment of equals and vertical equity demands unequal treatment of persons in different income, spending and wealth groups.[1] Much of the confusion and controversy in this respect arises only in the case of horizontal equity. It is unanimously held that present day income taxation does not satisfy the criterion of horizontal equity. It is an important issue involved in choosing appropriate tax bases. There is much less to be said and discussed about vertical equity as it is required whatever may be the tax base.

The Meade Committee Report points out: [2]

1. A good tax system should be horizontally equitable, i.e., it should treat like with the like.
2. It should be so constructed as to be capable of use for vertical redistribution between rich and poor.
3. There will be almost inevitably some clash between the criterion of economic efficiency (which will require low marginal rate of tax) and vertical redistribution (which will require high marginal rate of tax on the rich) but a good system is one that minimizes loss of efficiency.

---

1. Discussed in detail in the context of income and consumption bases.
2. *The Meade Committee Report,* Institute of Fiscal Studies, U.K., 1978.

Differential treatment of different categories of individuals justifies the need for more than one tax base and progression in the rates. Equity in the matters of taxation greatly depends upon how a tax base is defined and how the definition is put to practice. It also depends upon how differences between objective and subjective measurement of tax bases are reduced to a minimum. Objective definition and measurement of tax base are associated with accounting and subjective definition and measurement are associated with economic theory. Differences arise over the inclusion or exclusion of "accrued" and "realized" components of income. Much care should be exercised for the reason that from equity view-point, there should not be a wide difference between the definition of a tax base and its measurement. If in practice the base is different from the one defined, then there is every possibility of inequity creeping into the system. The moment it is so, then the tax system ceases to be "good".

2. *Efficiency*

The second important issue is that of efficiency. Tax system should be efficient in the sense that it should not adversely affect different incentives and initiatives.[3] Economists usually speak of income effect and substitution effect. One of the two operates when either rates are revised or some new taxes are introduced. The income effect is said to be present when a change in tax rate does not adversely affect desire to work hard, to earn, save and invest more than before. On the contrary, the substitution effect is said to be present when a change in tax rate discourages an individual from working hard and forces him to prefer leisure. It is also possible that by losing interest in work, he might reduce 'the effective supply of his labour'. This is for the reason that the labour does not mean merely physical exertion or presence at the work place but also a commitment to the assigned work. The other dimension of substitution effect is that a taxpayer, instead of reducing his labour, may report less income, consumption, wealth and business turnover simply to minimize his tax

3. Discussed in detail in the context of deadweight loss.

liability. This is a great possibility for the reason that a taxpayer normally does not have control over his own labour supply.

Economists usually approve income effect as it is not a symptom of economic inefficiency and waste. It is the only desired way of meeting additional tax liability. A strong income effect does good to both the taxpayers and national exchequer. In sharp contrast to this, the substitution effect stands for economic inefficiencies and waste. It deprives the taxpayer and national exchequer any additional advantage of more work effort and consequential high income.

Nevertheless, what is loss of efficiency? A tax is said to be inefficient when it loses neutrality. There is efficiency loss when:

1. The choice between present and future consumption is distorted.
2. The choice between labour and leisure is distorted.
3. The choice between two forms of investment is distorted.
4. The flow of return from different types of investment is distorted.
5. Tax considerations are more important than business and economic considerations.

It can be said that tax system ceases to be "good", "fair" and "efficient" when distortions as mentioned above occur.

3. *Simplicity*[4]

The final issue is that of simplicity. Tax system as prevailing in a country should be coherent, simple to understand and easy to administer. A taxpayer should know without much advice from the tax consultants as to how much tax he has to pay? Why should he pay tax? Moreover, what happens to the amount paid in tax? This will boost his confidence in the working of tax system and a taxpayer will

4. Many books on taxation make only a passing reference to this important issue. This issue is, therefore, studied in detail.

feel himself to be a part of whole system. Psychologically, this feeling works wonders. Simplicity is also desired to minimize cost of compliance, cost of record keeping, computing, reporting and planning.

Simplicity essentially depends upon an objective assessment of a tax base. This in turn depends upon clarity in the definition of a tax base. Difficulty arises in cases where major sources contributing to the base are not defined and measured objectively. Frequent and numerous changes in tax laws and their confusing interpretations by the courts of law make the system still more complicated. Unnecessary complexities erode the taxpayer's respect for and voluntary compliance with the law. Considerable time, resources and efforts are expended in understanding the tax laws and interpreting them in an attempt to minimize tax payments. The economic costs expressed in terms of time and fees paid to tax consultants are simply huge.

In order to simplify the tax system to the extent possible, governments usually make some *ad hoc* adjustments. These arrangements, however, do more damage than good. Normally, *ad hoc* measures are undertaken for some excellent reasons, for administrative convenience or to encourage deserving groups and worthy activities. Nevertheless, unfortunately, their overall impact seems to deprive the system of any consistent rationale or coherent structure.

We can identify three main factors contributing to the complexity of the tax system:

1. Computation on tax returns.
2. Measurement of tax base, inclusion and exclusion of different components of the base either partially or wholly.
3. Excessive tax planning to take advantage of different allowable deductions and tax concessions.

If the system is to be acceptable, it must be necessarily simple to understand and easy to administer. There should be a regular effort on the part of governments to simplify the tax system. For this purpose, one or two broad-based taxes with built-in adjustments are required. Above all, taxes should be used for the purpose of generating revenue only. These should not be used for non-revenue purposes which necessarily make the system to have more of tax related deductions and concessions.

Optimal Administration

The coverage of tax administration should be comprehensive and at the same time, the system as such should be closely integrated. The process of identifying taxpaying units and collection of revenue therefrom absorbs in itself, in costs, a good amount of revenue. In the context of the issue of simplicity, it is argued that the cost of collection should not be too "high". The question to examine here is: What kind of standard should be set for achieving optimality in administration?[5] Figure 3.1, which has three panels, provides a rough guideline for the principles to be followed. In each of the three panels, the horizontal axis measures units of tax administration, that is, the number of tax collectors needed.

Panel I shows that from economic efficiency viewpoint, it does not make sense to employ more than *N* tax collectors. The curve *MB* traces the marginal benefits from the work of tax collectors, which are expressed in terms of revenue collected. The declining *MB* curve is simply recognition of diminishing returns in tax collection. Tax collectors, however, do not work free. The *MC* curve shows the marginal costs associated with the employment of tax collectors. There is no reason to believe that the *MC* curve will not eventually slope upward. Panel I shows that the *(N+1)th* tax collector will cost more than he is worth.

Panels II and III put the problem in a different perspective. Panel II demonstrates that we normally do not expect to collect all the revenues that accrue. In other words, not all taxes due to taxpaying units are collected. After *N* units of tax administration, there is no significant change in revenue collected. Similarly, Panel III depicts that the administrative costs as a per cent of total tax collection rise steeply after *N* unit of tax administration.

5. Aronson, J. Richard, *Public Finance,* McGraw Hill, 1985, pp. 321-23.

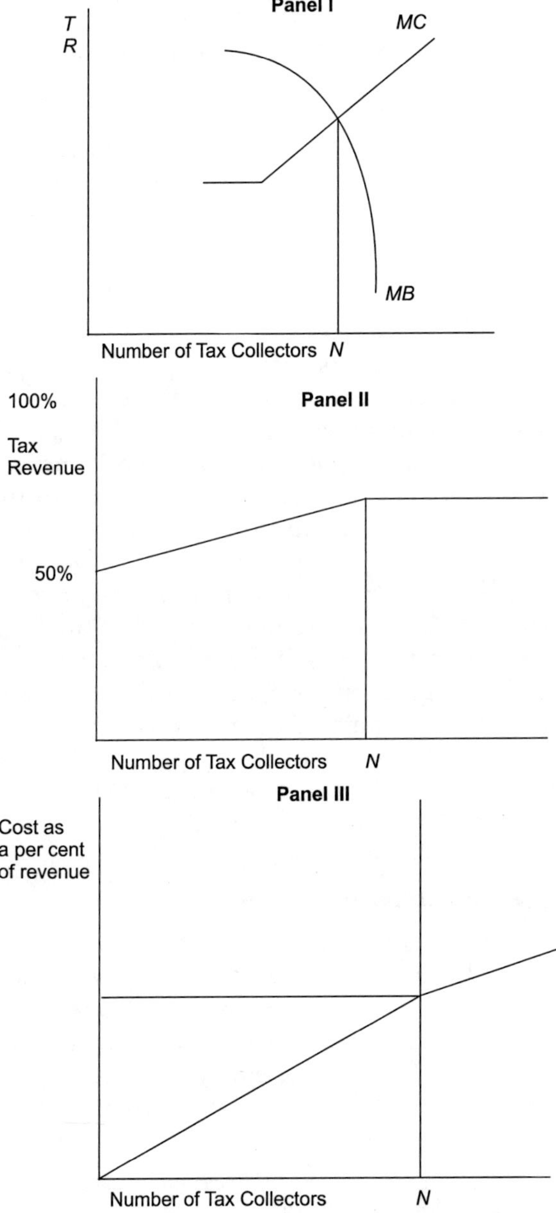

Fig. 3.1: Optimal Size of Tax Administration

To sum up, it can be said that normally the issues of equity, efficiency and administrative simplicity clash with one another. Efficiency and simplicity issues require less number of taxes with moderate rates. The notion of equity, on the contrary, demands a transfer of funds from private to public uses at progressive rates. As these notions are dynamic and relative as well, these are, therefore, highly debatable. The debate has generated an exciting branch of taxation known as "optimal taxation".

Costs of Taxation

Since long, economists have recognized the fact that taxation may have different types of costs, sometimes open and at others concealed. In his *Wealth of Nation*, [Book V, Chapter 2] Adam Smith has expounded some basic principles of taxation which provide an excellent introduction to the issues involved. With regard to the costs of taxation and the design of the tax system, Smith's first principle was as follows: "Every tax ought to be so contrived as both to take out and keep out of the pockets of the people as little as possible, over and above what it brings into the public treasury of the state." In other words, Smith is arguing here for the fact that taxes should be so designed as to minimize economic waste or to "take out and keep out of the pockets of the people as little as possible, over and above what the tax raises in revenue". The issue to examine here is: What kinds of costs did he have in mind? We can visualize the following major costs[6]:

1. *The Pure Economic Costs of Taxes*

Like many modern economists, Smith recognized that even if the tax system was simple, easy to comply with and easy to administer, it could still have economic costs in terms of excess burden or deadweight loss. By definition, it is the amount of money that is lost from the economy, in excess of what the government collects in revenue. Because it represents a loss to

---

6. Robson, Alex, *Taxation, Individual Incentives and Economic Growth*, Working Paper, School of Economics, Australian National University, Canberra, November, 2004.

the economy, it can be regarded as a dollar measure of the welfare costs of a tax.

2. *Administrative and Enforcement Costs*

Adam Smith in his book *Wealth of Nations* writes that: "The levying of [a tax] may require a great number of officers, whose salaries may eat up the greater part of the produce of the tax and whose perquisites may impose another additional tax upon the people." Presently tax systems not only require "a great number of officers", whose salaries do indeed "eat up the greater part of the produce of the tax" but many of the administrative costs have been transferred from the great number of officers to taxpayers themselves or to employers.

3. *Compliance Costs*

In the case of compliance costs Adam Smith remarks: "By subjecting the people to the frequent visits and the odious examination of the tax-gatherers, it may expose them to much unnecessary trouble, vexation, and oppression; and though vexation is not, strictly speaking, expense, it is certainly equivalent to the expense at which every man would be willing to redeem himself from it." In many cases, the administrative costs and compliance cost of taxation have become indistinguishable from one another, because responsibility of administration has been transferred to the private sector/ employer. For example, when employers withhold income taxes from employees, they are performing more of an administrative function than a compliance function. They are in effect collecting taxes on the government's behalf.

The growth of compliance costs manifests themselves in a variety of obvious ways, including the growth in the number of accountants, tax specialists and tax lawyers employed in the economy, many of who do not create any new wealth but are employed to prevent the government from acquiring the wealth of their clients.

The existence of complexity is itself an obstacle to tax reform and lower levels of taxation. It may be attributed to one interest group or another successfully lobbying for special deductions or treatment by the tax office. These special interest groups oppose reforms because complexity in certain parts of the tax code benefits them.

4. *Evasion Costs*

In the context of evasion costs, Adam Smith remarks: "An injudicious tax offers a great temptation to smuggling. But the penalties of smuggling must rise in proportion to the temptation. The law contrary to all the ordinary principles of justice, first creates the temptation, and then punishes those who yield to it and it commonly enhances the punishment, too, in proportions to the very circumstance which ought certainly to alleviate it, the temptation to commit the crime." Thus, according to Adam Smith, the taxation laws tempt people to evade taxes. Further, as and when caught in the process, they are penalized heavily. It may ruin unfortunate individuals who attempt unsuccessfully to evade the tax. It may put an end to the benefit which the community might have received from the productive employment of their capital. The evasion costs may also be understood in the context of parallel economy created on account of continuous evasion of taxes. In a large parallel economy, many government tools, including fiscal tools, lose their effectiveness.

5. *Rent Seeking Costs*

The revenues that governments raise from taxes represent lost consumption and profit opportunities for those economic actors who are taxed, but signify greater potential consumption and profit opportunities for those who gain access to this revenue by way of subsidies, direct transfers, or other redistributive government programmes. Interest groups may lobby the government in favour of high taxes in order to finance huge spending that might be directed their way. The subsidies, transfers, or other redistributive government policies are directed mainly at redistributing wealth rather than creating it. These represent additional social costs of establishing and increasing taxes and subsidies above and beyond the usual deadweight losses. The rent seeking activity is not directed at creating extra production, but instead aims at reducing output below its competitive level in some markets and increasing it in other markets.

In the following Chart 3.1, an attempt is made to show different types of costs of taxation.

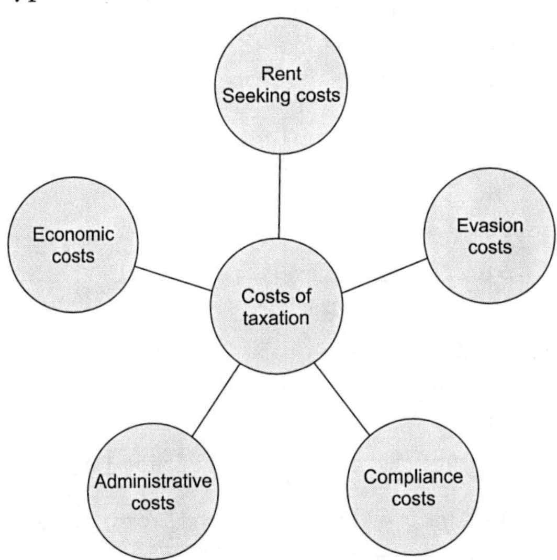

Chart 3.1: Costs of Taxation

In order to minimise the costs of taxation, economic or otherwise, it is necessary to have (i) a very effective tax administration and (ii) broad tax bases. How these two help in raising more revenue is illustrated with the help of Fig. 3.2.

In Fig. 3.2, tax effort and base are measured on the horizontal axis while tax revenue is measured on the vertical axis, where B and A represent the initial tax base and effort respectively that combine to yield R in revenue. Given this initial tax base, innovations in tax legislation that improve tax net, rate and structure and/or the effectiveness and efficiency of tax administration shifts the tax effort curve up to A_1 and tax revenue increases to R_1. Similarly, given the initial level of tax effort, an increase in the tax base to B_1 increases tax revenue but only to R_2. Thus, Fig. 3.2 seems to suggest that improvements in tax effort may be even more important in collecting more revenue out of the same base than growth in the base without improvements in tax effort, which is intuitive, plausible and sensible, since irrespective of the size of the tax base, zero effort brings in no revenue at all.[7] Of course, improvements in tax effort and growth in the tax base provide the best of the worlds for growth in tax revenue as these improvements are self-reinforcing such that revenue increases to R_3.

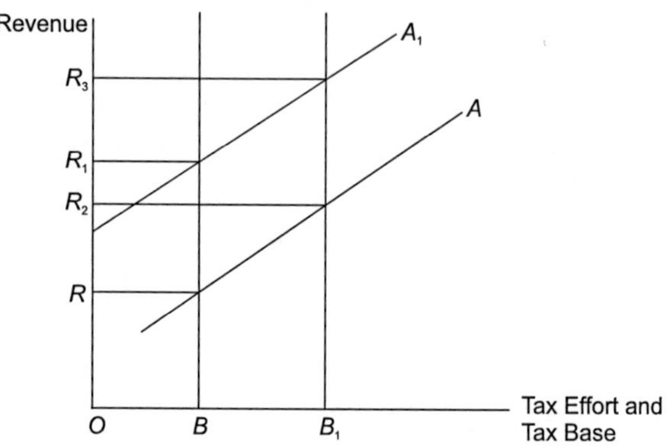

Fig. 3.2: Effective Administration and Broad Tax Base

Tax Expenditures

In addition to the mobilization of resources, the instrument of taxation is used for a variety of reasons. Among others, it is used for correcting personal disparities on one hand and regional disparities on the other. The correction of personal disparities calls for taxing the rich and then transferring resources in favour of poor. The correction of regional disparities calls for public-private participation in accelerating development. It requires huge investment, both at the public and private levels. Here, in order to attract investment, numerous tax concessions and exemptions are necessary. These are popularly known as tax expenditures. These assume the form of indirect tax subsidies. These occur when some fiscal advantage is conferred on a group of individuals or a particular

7. Botlhole, T.D. and T.J. Agiobenebo, "The Tax Elasticity and Buoyancy of the Bostwana Tax System and Their Determinants", *The ICFAI Journal of Financial Economics,* Vol. IV, No. 4, December, 2006, pp. 53-54.

activity by reducing tax liability rather than by direct cash subsidy.

Both, tax concessions and cash subsidies have much in common. They allow the government to favour certain groups or activities and they both require the level of taxation on others to be higher or public expenditure on alternative projects to be lower than would otherwise be the case.[8] In one way or the other, tax expenditures can be related to tax avoidance which can be summarized as follows[9]:

Table 3.1: Tax Evasion and Avoidance

Evasion	By Commission	Intentional/Unintentional
	By Omission	Intentional Unintentional
Avoidance	Legal loopholes disapproved of by government	
	Tax expenditures as a part of approved government policy	

The U.S. Congressional Joint Committee on Taxation defines tax expenditures as under: "Special income tax provisions are referred to as tax expenditures because they are considered to be analogous to direct outlay programmes. Tax expenditures are most similar to those direct spending programmes which have no spending limits and which are available as entitlements." [10]

Tax expenditures arise on account of: (1) errors, (2) less than tight drafting of the tax legislation, (3) as a deliberate policy to encourage a particular activity.[11] The effect of a good or service being untaxed *vis-à-vis* others can be understood with the help of Fig. 3.3.

The curve *AB* is the initial budget line. If both *Y* (all other goods and services) and *X* are taxed, the budget constraint moves towards the origin in a parallel fashion *CD*. The post-tax equilibrium combination of purchases is determined at

8. James, Simon and Christopher Nobes, *The Economics of Taxation*, Philip Allan Publishers Limited, 1978, pp. 41-43.
9. Cullis, John and Philip Jones, *Public Finance and Public Choice*, Oxford University Press, 1998, pp. 192-93.
10. http://www.ctj.org
11. Cullis, John and Philip Jones, *op. cit.*, p. 192.

point *e*. If *X* is exempted either by accidental or deliberate action, the budget constraint becomes *CB*. In the event, equilibrium is at point e_1 while consumption of *X* increasing. The tax raised is measured by the vertical distance at point *e* between *AB* and *CB*. The drawback of *X* being untaxed is revealed if outcome at *e* is compared with one that raises the same tax but with no exemptions. The budget line *EF* through e_1 allows a higher indifference curve to be achieved without affecting revenue outcome.

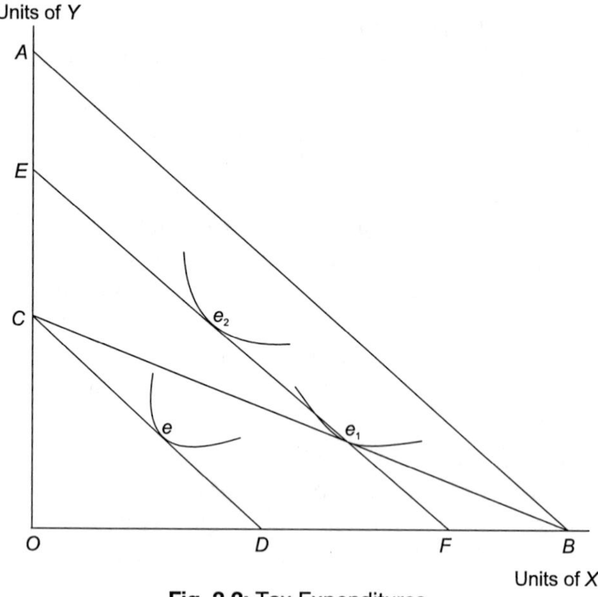

Fig. 3.3: Tax Expenditures

In case of tax expenditures, certain difficulties can be noticed. First, subsidies through a tax expenditure programme are relatively hidden. When the government provides cash aid, the figures are known and, therefore, liable for scrutiny. These are open to debate, review and possible alteration at regular intervals. This is not so for tax expenditures which remain comparatively hidden. Secondly, tax expenditures are not worth the same to different people. People with low income do not gain any benefit from deductions against tax. Further, the benefit in tax saved is huge for individuals subject to high rates of tax. Thirdly, tax expenditures complicate the tax system itself. Finally, these fuel corruption because in the absence of a proper drafting of laws their interpretations might be different.

The issue of tax expenditures should also be examined in the context of universal tax reform in the areas of personal and corporate income taxation. The hallmark here, over the last two decades, is an across the board reduction in tax rates. In order to avoid any adverse impact of a reduction in rates on tax revenues, it is necessary to re-examine the whole gamut of deductions and concessions. These need to be re-examined in order to improve tax-GDP ratio.

The multitude of tax expenditures is affecting revenue collection adversely. Therefore, like other spending programmes, the tax expenditures should also be evaluated on the following grounds:

1. Is the subsidy designed to serve an important public purpose?
2. Is the subsidy actually helping to achieve its goals?
3. Are the benefits, if any, from the subsidy commensurate with its cost?
4. Are the benefits of the subsidy fairly distributed or they disproportionately targeted to those who do not need or deserve government assistance?
5. Is the subsidy well-administered?

Of late, governments all over the world have realized the magnitude of revenue leakage on account of tax expenditures. The popular notion is that the subsidies for poor should continue, exemptions for rich should be scrapped. Table 3.2 shows the revenue forgone in India on account of multitude of exemptions allowed.[12]

12. http://www.ctj.org

Table 3.2: Exemptions and Revenue Forgone (2004-05)

Exemptions	Revenue Forgone in Rs. Crore
Corporate Income	57,852
Personal Income	11,695
Cooperatives	1,534
Excise duty	30,449
Customs duty	92,561
Export Credit	35,430

Source: Ministry of Finance

A news report published in *India Today* [12-02-07] maintains that in voluminous budget documents is buried a startling disclosure that for every two rupees the government collects in taxes, it forgoes one to the multitude of tax exemptions. In 2004-05, the Ministry of Finance collected Rs. 3,03,037 crore. Exemptions robbed the exchequer of Rs. 1,58,661 crore, with which the collection would have touched Rs. 4,61,698 crore. Last year, in the garb of investments in backward regions, companies with taxable income of more than 500 crore claimed exemptions to pay 16 per cent in taxes whereas the benchmark tax rate for top corporations is 33 per cent. The details of revenue forgone in the years 2007-08 and 2008-09 are startling and at the same time worrying. The revenue forgone as a per cent of total tax collection has increased from 48.16 per cent in 2007-08 to 68.95 per cent in 2008-09. All this is clear from Table 3.3.

Table 3.3: Amount of Revenue Forgone in 2007-08 and 2008-09

(Rs. crore)

Sl. No.	Tax	Revenue forgone 2007-08	Revenue forgone as a per cent of total tax collection	Revenue forgone 2008-09	Revenue forgone as a per cent of total tax collection 2008-09
1.	Corporate Income Tax	62199	10.50	68914	11.36
2.	Personal Income Tax	38057	6.43	39553	6.52

(Contd.)

3.	Excise duty	87468	14.77	128293	21.16
4.	Customs duty	153593	25.95	225752	37.23
5.	Total	341317	57.67	462512	76.28
6.	Less Export Credit	56265	9.50	44417	7.32
7.	Grand Total	285052	48.16	418095	68.95

Source: Budget Document 2009-10, Table 12

The question why tax expenditures rather than direct and open subsidies are used is interesting.[13] It may be for a variety of reasons. A few important are cited as under:

(1) It may be that politicians prefer not to be seen spending public money, and so they hide behind the veil of tax expenditures.

(2) Tax expenditures may be a device to earn political support of big taxpayers and corporate houses. Here unscrupulous politicians can have their cake and eat it too.

(3) It may be that tax expenditures are convenient a tool for those wishing to manipulate pattern and flow of investment in the economy.

(4) Pressure groups and lobbies also play an important role.

(5) Rent seeking activities further promote tax expenditures.

Whatever may be the reason, it is clear that the issue of tax expenditures deserves more attention than it has received to date. It is necessary that the taxpayers in particular and public in general should be informed of the consequences of ever increasing tax expenditures. Serious studies, both at the micro and macro levels need to be conducted.

---

13. James, Simon and Christopher Nobes, *op. cit.*, p. 43.

Excess Burden of Taxation

4

Objective: To study the notion of excess burden of taxation popularly known as deadweight loss or efficiency cost.

Organization: The concept; fundamental to public finance; neutral tax; different types of elasticity of demand and supply; measurement of excess burden and significance.

The Concept

The concept of excess tax burden may be related to the observations of Adam Smith [Book V, Ch. II] that taxation may "obstruct the industry of the people; taxes are frequently so much more burdensome to the people than they are beneficial to the sovereign". In modern literature on taxation, Adam Smith's remarks form the base of a study of distortion of individuals' choices between goods, or producers' choices between factors, and so impose an additional burden on the taxpaying community. The earliest example cited in this connection is from Great Britain where in 1747, many taxpayers decided to avoid the window tax by bricking up their windows. The lack of amenity arising from the blocking of windows was clearly a cost of the window tax; but although it was a cost to the taxpayer, it was of no benefit to the government either. This type of the cost may be described considering the interaction of supply and demand in a hypothetical market. The demand curve is a normal downward sloping demand curve. The supply curve, however, is vertical, that is, it has a price elasticity of 0. The equilibrium price in this market is P_e and Q_e is the equilibrium output.

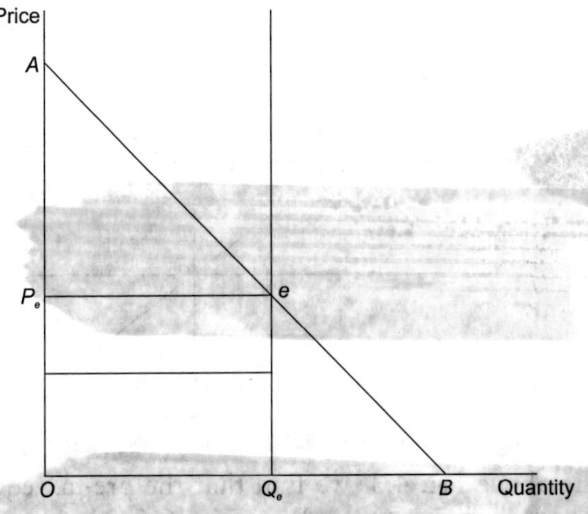

Fig. 4.2: A Neutral Tax

Thus, OP_eOQ_e represents the total gross receipts associated with the item. A tax, which took 50 per cent of OP_eOQ_e, would have no effect on P_e or Q_e. Some might argue that such a tax might not be fair, but there can be no complaining that such would have unwanted side effects. Since the price of the item has not been changed in relation to competing or complementary goods, there is no reason to believe that consumer choice is distorted by the tax.

An understanding of the above Fig. 4.2 helps us appreciate why land taxation has been a favourite form as suggested by economists. Land is that factor of production whose supply is perfectly inelastic in the long-run as well as in the short-run. Tax on land cannot reduce its supply; neither will a tax on land change its productivity and therefore, the demand for it.

Elastic and Inelastic Demand

Let us consider two cases where demand for a product is elastic in one case and inelastic in the other. The demand schedule for X is shown as DK, while SV is the supply schedule.

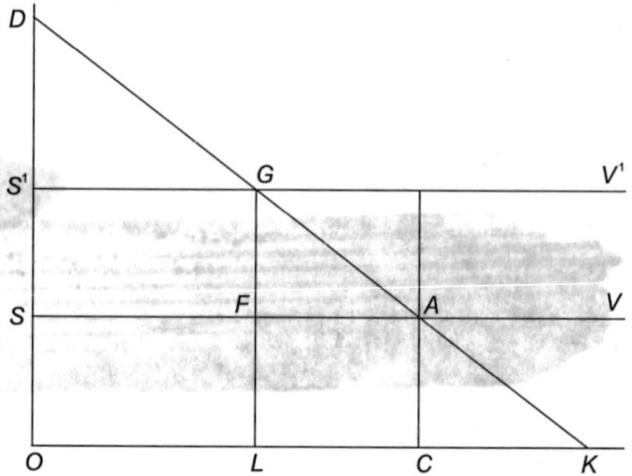

Fig. 4.3: Case I: Elastic Demand for Product *X*

In the above Fig. 4.3, we find that the pre-tax equilibrium is at A, the price being OS and quantity OC. Now a unit of tax $u = SS^1$ is imposed. As this tax is added to the cost, the supply schedule rises to S^1V^1 and the new equilibrium is at G. The gross price (inclusive of tax) rises to OS^1 while output fall to OL and tax revenue equals SS^1GF. Since we are dealing with a case of constant cost, consumers bear the entire burden, defined as SS^1GF and equal to revenue. Whereas, prior to tax, they would have paid $OSFL$ for the amount OL, they must now pay OS^1GL, the additional amount being SS^1GF, or tax revenue.

This, however, is not a complete description of the consumer burden. Prior to tax, consumers paid $OSAC$ for amount OC but would have been willing to pay $ODAC$. Since all units under competitive pricing are priced at their marginal value, consumers received a "consumer surplus" equal to the difference between actual value and potential payment or SDA. Under the tax, their consumer surplus has been reduced to S^1DG. They have thus suffered a loss of surplus equal to SS^1GA. Of this, SS^1GF is offset by the government's revenue gain, but the triangle *FGA* remains a deadweight loss or excess burden to the economy.

What determines the magnitude of the excess burden? As may be seen by rotating *DK* around point *A* as the pivot, the triangle *FGA* becomes smaller as demand becomes less elastic. We may now compare the excess burden if equal revenue is obtained from product *X* (case I) the demand for which is moderately inelastic and from product *Z* (case II), the demand schedule for which is highly inelastic as is shown in Fig. 4.4. Pre-tax quantity and price are the same in both cases, but the unit tax *FG* needed for yield SS^1GF is less for Z than for X. We also note that for *Z*, where demand is highly inelastic, the excess burden *FGA* is smaller.

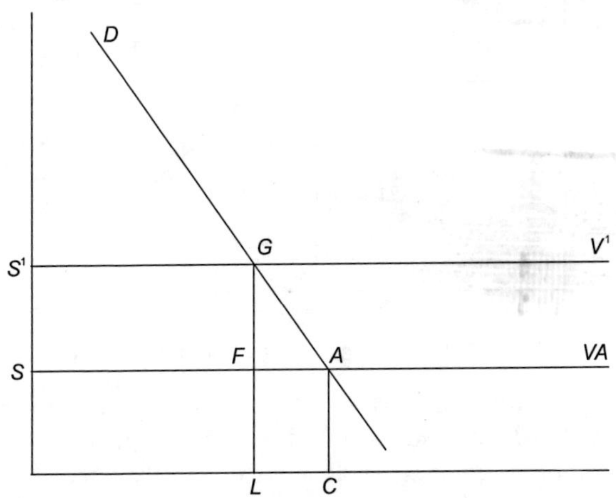

Fig. 4.4: Case II: Inelastic Demand for Product *Z*

Normal Demand and Supply Curves

The Fig. 4.5 shows the impact of a tax in a market containing both a normal downward-sloping demand curve and a normal upward-sloping supply curve. The tax will raise revenue, it will affect equilibrium prices and quantities, and it will produce an excess burden.[5]

5. Aronson, Richard J., *op. cit.*, p. 317.

The pre-tax equilibrium occurs at price *Pe* and quantity *Qe*. There is a consumer surplus of *ABPe*. A unit of tax of *CG* will result in a new higher equilibrium price at *P′e* and the new lower equilibrium quantity at *Q′e*. The amount of consumer surplus associated with the new equilibrium is *ACP′e*. Thus, the imposition of the tax has resulted in a loss of consumer surplus of *Pe P′e CB*.

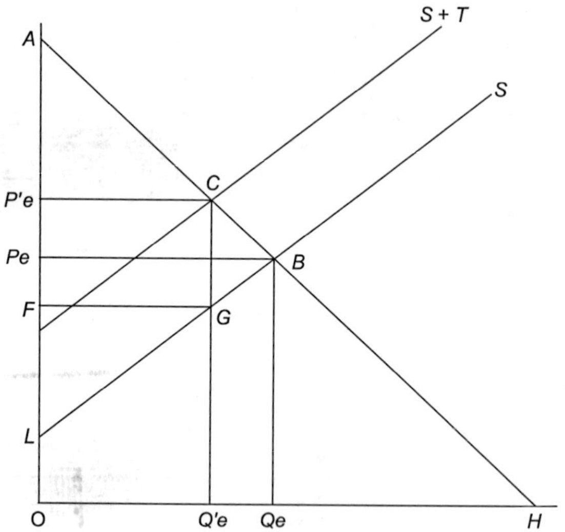

Fig. 4.5: Normal Demand and Supply Curves

Another kind of loss of surplus has occurred as well. The area *PeBL* measures what is called producer surplus. Diagrammatically, the area above the supply curve but below the price per unit line, producer surplus, is equivalent to the profit and rent generated in this market. Because of the imposition of a tax, the net price to the producer will fall from *Pe* to *F*. At the new equilibrium quantity *Q′e*, the amount of producer surplus becomes *LFG*. Thus, the tax has resulted in a diminution of producer surplus equal to *PeFGB*.

The combined loss of consumers and producer surplus can now be compared to the volume of tax revenues generated by a unit of *CG*. The excess of lost consumer and producer surplus over tax revenues *(Pe P'e CB + PeFGB) – P'e CGF* is equal to *CBG*, the excess burden or deadweight loss caused by the tax.

Perfectly Inelastic Demand Curve

Let us now examine the case of a market demand which is perfectly inelastic. Here, we have perfectly vertical demand curve *AH* and a pretax equilibrium at P_e, Q_e. The imposition of a unit *CB* raises the equilibrium price by an equivalent amount to the level of P_e'. The tax revenue collected is equal to $P_e P_e' CB$. Since, in this case, the loss of consumer surplus is just equal to the tax revenues, there is no excess burden. That is, zero elasticity of supply and zero elasticity of demand imply the absence of excess burden of tax or deadweight loss. By comparing Fig. 4.4 with Fig. 4.5, we see the influence of demand elasticity on the magnitude of the welfare loss. Greater the elasticity, higher is the welfare loss.

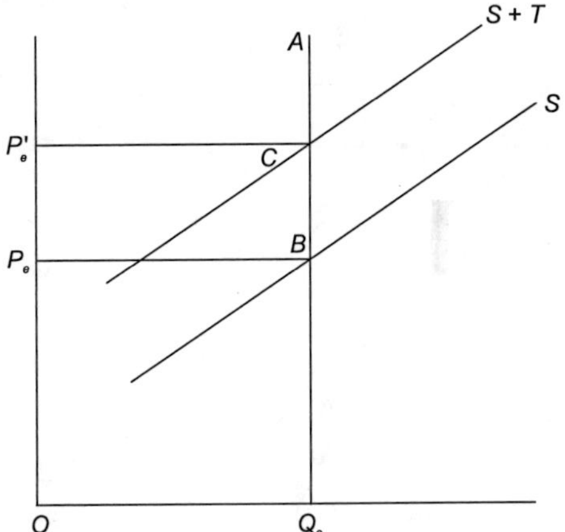

Fig. 4.6: Perfectly Inelastic Demand Curve

Income Taxes versus Excise Taxes

In the discussion of excess tax burden, it is generally observed that the income taxes are superior to excise taxes. This proposition was put forward by Hicks [1939] and Joseph [1939] that income taxes impose a lower excess burden than taxes on specific goods, and income taxes do not distort consumer choices between goods.[6] It is assumed that perfect competition prevails, that there are no external effects and that a Pareto-efficient allocation of resources exists before either tax is imposed. It is assumed that the supply of factors of production is fixed and that these factors are fully employed both before and after either the income tax or the excise tax is imposed. Further, we suppose that the same amount of revenue has to be raised by whichever tax is used and that the pattern of government spending is the same in both cases. The taxes will be applied to a simple two-goods (*X* and *Y*) model. Finally, it is assumed that the choice of tax is between a commodity tax, which is levied on good *X* but not on *Y* and a proportional income tax which is levied on all incomes. In Fig. 4.7 the pretax budget line is *AB*. A consumer will choose that combination of *X* and *Y* which enables him to reach his highest possible indifference curve, given the budget constraint.

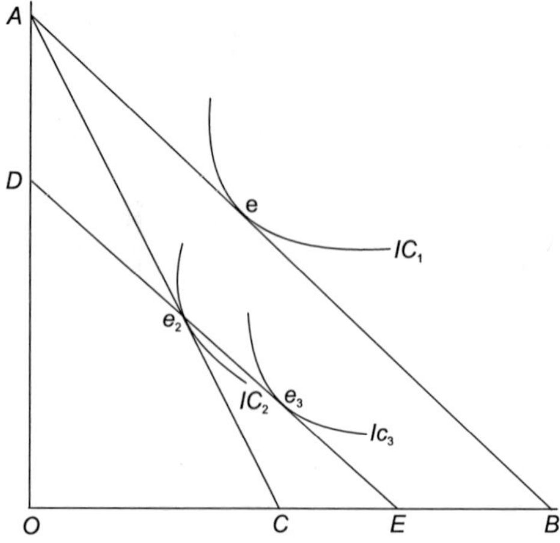

Fig. 4.7: Income vs. Excise Taxes

A specific excise tax levied on commodity *X* has the effect of shifting the consumer's budget constraint from *AB* to *AC*. It must swivel in this way because if our individual consumed only *Y*, he is able to buy the same amount as before. Given the budget constraint of *AC*, the highest attainable indifference

6. James, Simon and Christopher Nobes, *op. cit.*, p. 24.

curve is now IC_2. If an income tax is imposed instead, the effect is also to shift the budget constraint inwards. The income tax does not distort the consumer's choice between X and Y and so their relative prices must remain the same. To yield the equal revenue as under an excise tax, the new budget line DE must be parallel to AB. The tax simply reduces his income so that he can afford less of both. As the income tax is required to raise the same revenue as the excise tax, DE will pass though e_2 so that the individual is left with sufficient income to be able to buy the same combination of goods, irrespective of the tax to which he is subjected. However, with a budget line DE, he can attain the higher indifference curve of IC_3. As compared to earlier, he is clearly better off on IC_3 than on IC_2. On the basis of assumption listed above, it may be argued that an income tax inflicts less excess burden on the taxpayer than a specific excise tax of equal yield. It does so simply because it interferes less with consumer choice and allocation of resources.

It should be noted here that the argument as developed above depends on the indirect tax being imposed on X but not on Y. If the tax were levied on both goods, the analysis would be the same as that for an income tax.

Choice between Goods and Leisure

A similar analysis applies to a tax on wage income and the choice between goods and leisure.[7] To focus on this aspect, we now assume that there is only one consumer good (a composite of goods X and Z) and once more take the choice between present and future consumption as fixed. The resulting excess burden is shown in the following Fig. 4.8.

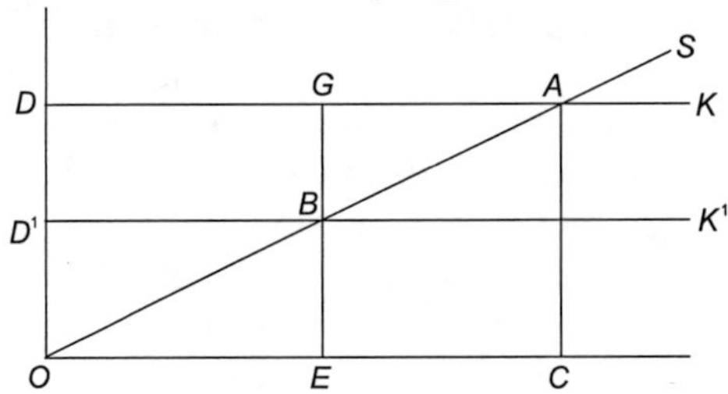

Fig. 4.8: Choice between Goods and Leisure

7. Musgrave, Richard A., *op. cit.*, p. 282.

Let *OS* be the supply schedule of labour and *DK* be the demand schedule. The pre-tax equilibrium is at *A*, while hours worked are *OC* and the wage rate is equal to *OD*. We assume an infinitely elastic demand for labour. As a tax on wage income is imposed at a rate D^1D/OD, the net demand schedule drops down to D^1K^1. The new equilibrium is at *B*, with hours worked falling to *OE* and the net wage to OD^1. Tax revenue equals D^1DGB and the entire burden is borne by worker. Once more this is not the entire story. Prior to imposition of the tax, hours *OC* were worked at a wage *OD* and total wages paid were *ODAC*. But workers would have been willing to offer their labour at a wage bill equal to *OAC*. *ODA* was thus a rent or supplier surplus. After tax this surplus declines to OD^1B. The decline in surplus thus equals D^1DAB. Of this, D^1DGB is offset by the gain in revenue, leaving the triangle *BGA* as the net loss or excess burden. The burden will be smaller the less elastic supply schedule.

Choice between Present and Future Consumption

The same argument as above may be applied for tax on interest and its effect on the supply of saving. Returning to Fig. 4.8 as above, we now measure the rate of interest on the vertical axis and saving on the horizontal axis. Prior to tax, borrowers are willing to pay interest rate *OD* and saving equals *OC*. When a tax at rate D^1D/OD is imposed, the net demand schedule drops to D^1K^1 and saving falls to *OE*. Revenue equals D^1DGB, the saver's loss of surplus equals D^1DAB, and the excess burden equals *BGA*.

How to Measure the Excess Burden of a Tax?

A study of measurement of excess tax burden is important for two reasons.[8] First, the deadweight loss inherent in alternative taxes should be considered in constructing a good tax system. Secondly, the deadweight loss of marginal tax dollar in such a system must be known to determine the proper size of budget, because it sets the cost (tax dollar plus deadweight loss) which need be measured against the benefits derived from the marginal expenditure dollar.

8. Mursgrave, Richard A. and Pebby Musgrave, *Public Finance in Theory and Practice*, *op. cit.*, p. 293.

How can the excess burden of a tax, defined above, be measured, that is, be expressed in some equivalent monetary units? For simplicity sake, the case of a single taxed commodity is considered. The popular measure is that of Dupuit-Marshall-Harberger. This measure of tax burden relies on the use of concept of consumer's surplus as a measure of the consumer's net welfare in consuming a commodity. In the following Fig. 4.9 the consumer's ordinary demand curve for commodity X, with X_o being the quantity demanded at the initial price P_o with no tax.

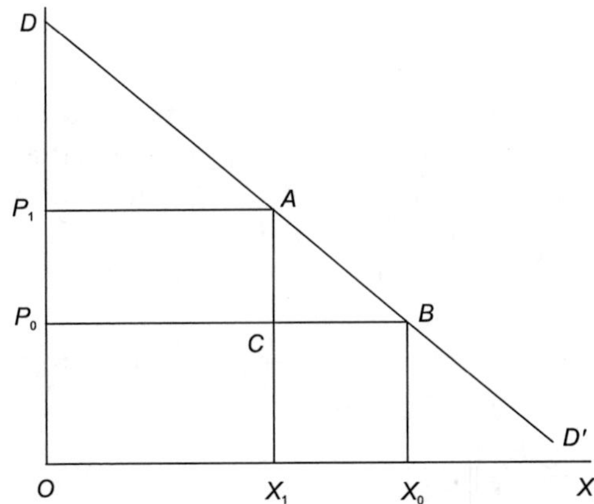

Fig. 4.9: Measurement of Excess Burden

The consumer's surplus is then the familiar area below the demand curve but above the price line, that is, the area of the triangle DP_oB. Consider now a tax at the *ad valorem* rate t is imposed on X, so that its consumer price rises to $P_1 = (1 + t).P_o$, resulting in a decrease in the quantity of X demanded from X_o to X_1. Compared with the pre-tax situation, consumer surplus has now declined by the area of the trapezoid P_1ABP_o. The area of the rectangle P_1ACP_o represents, however, the total tax payment. Hence, the excess burden of the tax is that area of the triangle ABC, which measures the excess of the reduction in consumes surplus above and beyond that is due to the tax payment.

Mrs. Ursula Hicks in her work *Public Finance* [1947] reaches the conclusion that the excess burden varies directly with the elasticity of supply and demand of the taxed product or factor.[9] Earlier, Ramsey had remarked that if "a given revenue is to be raised by proportionate taxes on some or all uses of income, the taxes on different uses being possibly at different rates; how should these rates be adjusted in order that the decrement of utility may be minimal".[10] To this poser, Pigou pointed out that "the best way of raising a given revenue is by a system of taxes, under which the rates become progressively higher as we pass from uses of very elastic demand or supply to uses where demand or supply are progressively less elastic".[11]

There is much controversy in the literature about the D-M-H measure of excess burden. At the root of the controversy is the question concerning the validity of using the concept of consumer's surplus as a measure of consumer net welfare. To circumvent the problem of D-M-H measure, Hicks proposed replacing the use of ordinary curves with compensated demand curves.

The following formula has been developed to measure the excess burden associated with a tax[12]:

$$W = \frac{1}{2}\left[\frac{E_d E_s}{E_d + E_s}\right] t^2 PQ$$

Where

W = excess burden

E_d = elasticity of demand

E_s = elasticity of supply

t = tax rate

PQ = outlays on goods or item inclusive of tax.

This formula provides a valuable insight into the practical problems of building tax structure. The excess burden rises

9. Hicks, Ursula, *Public Finance,* Pitman Publishing Corporation, New York, 1947, pp. 167-72.

10. Ramsey Frank, "A Contribution to the Theory of Taxation", *Economic Journal*, Vol. 37, No. 145, 1927, pp. 46-61.

11. For further details one may refer to A.C. Pigou's *A Study in Public Finance*, Macmillan & Co., Ltd., London, 1951, pp. 104-06.

12. Aronson, J. Richard, *op. cit.*, pp. 320-21.

with the square of the tax rate. Thus, roughly speaking, we have a reason for preferring abroad-based tax to set off more narrowly defined taxes. In the following Fig. 4.10 the tax revenues (*TR*) are measured on the vertical axis and the size of the tax base on the horizontal axis. Ot_1 shows the total amount of revenue that is raised by applying a tax rate of t_1 to tax bases of different sizes. Ot_2 and Ot_3 show the revenue that is generated by applying higher tax rates than t_1, e.g., $t_3 > t_2 > t_1$.

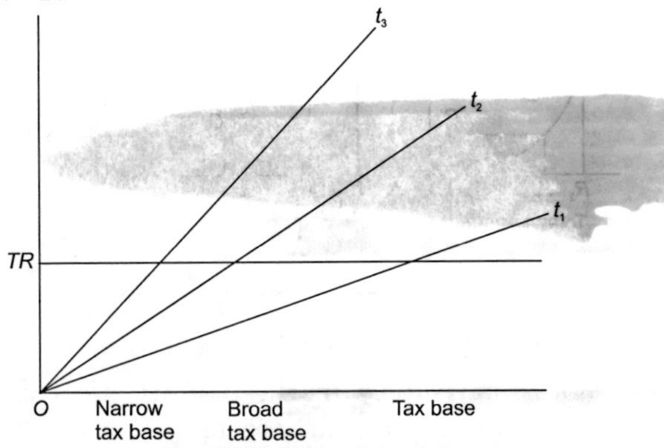

Fig. 4.10: Excess Burden and Tax Rates

The Fig. 4.10 shows that there are several ways to raise the amount of total revenue *TR*. We can use a high tax rate on a narrow base or a low rate on a broad base. However, since the lower rate on the broad base can be expected to produce a smaller excess burden, it is the one to be favoured.

The analysis of optimal tax is, however, very sophisticated.[13] Empirical measurements of the magnitude of efficiency costs are difficult, with estimates varying widely for different taxes and suggesting an overall burden equal to perhaps 15 per cent of revenue for the average tax dollar and substantially higher for the marginal tax dollar.[14]

13. For basic readings, one may refer to A.B. Atkinson and J.E. Stiglitz *Lectures in Public Economics,* Amaresh Bagchi *Readings in Public Finance*, David Bradford and Harvey S. Rosen *The Optimal Taxation of Commodities and Income,* David Newberry and Nicholas Stern *The Theory of Taxation for Developing Countries,* and many others.
14. Musgrave, Richard A. and Pebby Musgrave, *Public Finance in Theory and Practice*, *op. cit.*, p. 296.

Side Effects and Excess Burden

The following Fig. 4.11 depicts a situation in which demand *AD* is of normal shape but in which the supply curve is perfectly elastic.

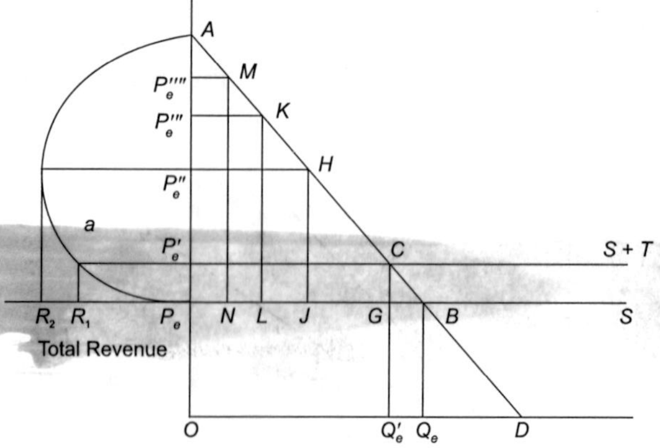

Fig. 4.11: Excess Burden and Tax Rate—Tax Revenue Curve

The horizontal supply means that we are considering an item that is reproducible at constant cost. The before-tax equilibrium in a competitive market for such an item occurs at price P_e and quantity Q_e. Assume now that a unit tax of *CG* is placed on the object. As long as the supplier's view of how much money they want for their goods remains unchanged, the supply situation can now be viewed as the line *S+T*.

The effect of the tax is dramatically different from that which occurred when the supply was perfectly inelastic. Here, the new equilibrium price P'_e will be higher than before and the new equilibrium quantity Q'_e will be less than before. The tax has generated revenue equal to $P_e P'_e\ CG$ but also produced a side effect. The price of the item has been increased and this can be expected to induce consumers to substitute less preferred substitute for the taxed item.

Two additional points are worthy of note here.[15] The first is the relationship between the tax rate and the amount of tax revenue. A tax at the rate of *CG* per unit produces a tax

15. Aronson, J. Richard, *op. cit.*, pp. 314-15.

revenue of $P_e P_e' CG = R_1$. This is shown at a point on the left-hand portion of Fig. 4.11. A tax rate of zero would, of course, produce no revenue. Thus, the curve segment $P_e a$ begins to race out a relationship that might be called a "tax rate-revenue" curve. Will higher tax rates always result in greater revenues? A glance at Fig. 4.11 will show that this not to be expected. Geometrically, tax revenues are represented by the area of the rectangle touching the line of segment AB. It is obvious that at the tax rate HJ, which is higher than CG, the volume of tax revenues will also be higher. The area of $P_e P_e' HJ$ is greater than the area $P_e P_e' CG$. It is also obvious, however, that at tax rates yet higher, like KL and MN, the amount collected in revenues will fall off. That is, the area $P_e P_e''' MN$ is smaller than the areas $P_e P_e'' HJ$.

In general, tax revenues will be maximised at that point along the demand curve where the percentage increase in the tax rate is equal to the percentage reduction in the tax base. The curve $P_e acA$ describes the full relationship. No revenue will be collected at zero rates and also when the tax rate is 100 per cent.

In recent years, the rate-revenue curve between income tax rates and revenues has been dramatized by Arthur Laffer, in the popular press, has even been referred to as the "Laffer Curve". The relationship is important to remember. The constant reminder should be that excessively high tax rates can produce less revenue as well as serious side effects in the form of excess burden.

A further insight provided by Fig. 4.11 comes from the considering the meaning of the area CBG. This amount represents an excess burden or deadweight loss caused by a tax. It is the loss in welfare caused by the unwanted side effects. Before the imposition of a tax, the amount of consumer surplus is ABP_e. After the imposition of the tax, the equilibrium price rises to P_e', the equilibrium quantity fall to Q_e' and the amount of consumer surplus fall to ACP_e'. Thus, the loss of consumer surplus due to the tax is equal to $P_eP_e'CB$. The tax does, however, generate revenues equal to $P_eP'CG$. The difference between the loss of consumer surplus and the volume of tax revenues, $P_eP_e'CB$ minus $P_eP_e'CG$, is the excess burden, CBG, or deadweight loss due to that tax.

It is now important to compare Fig. 4.1 with Fig. 4.11. In Fig. 4.1, there is no deadweight loss or excess burden associated with the tax. There is no loss in consumer surplus and the amount of tax revenues is just equal to the loss in producer surplus. This occurs because in Fig. 4.1, the supply curve had zero elasticity, and, thus, a neutral tax can now be described as one which has no side effects and produces no excess or deadweight loss. Other things being constant, it appears from the efficiency point of view that taxes on items of inelastic supply are to be preferred to taxes with elastic supply.

Conclusion

The study of excess burden has considerable academic and practical value. It provides a general warning that policies that erode the tax base and therefore increase the tax rate and burden need very special justification. Furthermore, tax-financed expenditure and redistribution policies must provide benefits that outweigh the efficiency costs of raising the required revenue. The excess burden of taxation provides a benchmark with which to measure public projects or policy interventions against. From an efficiency point of view, any project or policy that fails to offset the cost of taxation should not be undertaken.

It also suggests that a tax system which has a broad tax base is likely to impose less excess burden than a tax with a narrow base. If the collection of tax is spread over a large number of goods and activities, then generally it will interfere less with consumer choice than if taxes were concentrated on a smaller areas of the economy.

The practical application of deadweight loss concept associated with taxation is to minimize tax levels whilst maximizing the benefits of public sector outputs. Supporters of collective action through public sector naturally emphasize the wider benefits of public services whilst supporters of free-markets would naturally emphasize inefficiencies.

Basis for Taxation: Income

5

Objective: To examine suitability of income base.

Organization: Types of taxes; history of income tax; defining income; income tax and equity; different equity-related problems; root cause.

Types of Taxes

Today, the overall tax system consists of direct and indirect taxes. Importance of the two, their composition, degree of progression and their responsiveness varies from one country to the other. In developed countries, the direct taxes contribute more to the national exchequer and in developing countries, the proportion of tax revenue raised through indirect taxes is high. It is altogether a different question as to why the tax pattern differs. A number of sociological, historical, political and economic factors have contributed to the differences in tax patterns. It is, however, realized that excessive reliance should not be placed on indirect taxes.

Of course, the coverage of indirect taxes happens to be broad but these are mainly proportional and possibility of any progression is at the best very limited. These cannot be adjusted to the personal circumstances of an individual taxpayer. The burden of indirect taxes is shifted forward and an indiscriminate use of indirect taxes causes cost-price escalations. A number of studies have pointed out their inherent inflationary potential. Direct taxes, on the other hand, are preferred on the grounds of equity and efficiency. As against indirect taxes, direct taxes are personalized. Their rate structure may be made progressive so as to raise a required amount of revenue. These are not generally shifted forward. Further, direct taxes are regarded as the most powerful weapon in the fiscal armory of the state to curb the income-consumption-wealth inequalities. Greater the desire to take into account unitary differences (e.g., family size, age and state of health) in distributing the tax burden, the more crucial it is to impose taxes at the personal level.

The present system of direct taxes is primarily income-based, be it personal income, corporate income, windfalls, agricultural income, transfer income, rent, interest, *et al.* Income is generally regarded as a convenient index of ability to pay. Each taxpayer is asked to pay according to his ability to pay expressed in terms of income earned. The substitutes to income base are consumption and wealth. Whereas consumption-based indirect taxes are prevalent in all countries of the world, a direct personal consumption-based expenditure tax is conspicuous by its absence. The expenditure tax, as suggested by Kaldor had a very small yet bitter debut in India and Sri Lanka.

In a number of countries, wealth tax is in operation not as a substitute to income tax but as its supplement. A supplemental wealth tax is favoured on the ground that the income tax of its own is not sufficient to achieve vertical equity. Wealth is not without its advantages. It confers to its owner a control over economic resources which could be further used to accumulate still more wealth. It enables its owner to take advantage of economic opportunities that may arise. Given the imperfections in both money and capital markets, it is often not possible for individuals to take advantage of changing market conditions without adequate wealth. In case of companies, wealthy shareholders are in a position to exercise considerable influence over policies. Above all, the advantage of status that wealth bestows on its owner is no less important. It is to tax these advantages that a supplemental wealth tax is desired alongside.

The following Table 5.1 gives a fair idea of different taxes, direct and indirect, and their respective bases.

Table 5.1: Types of Broad-based Taxes

Tax Base	Personal form	Indirect or *ad valorem*
Income	Personal income tax	Employees payroll tax, corporate income tax, value added tax (income based) interest tax
Wealth	Annual net worth tax	Property tax
Consumption	Spendings or expenditure tax	Sales tax, value added tax (consumption base)

It is important to recognize that the size of major tax bases, income, consumption and wealth are not strictly independent of one other. They are related and this means that taxing one can be expected to influence the size of another. We must also recognize that the amount and value of our assets depends upon the volume of saving and investment. The growth of a society's wealth depends on people's willingness to save and invest. There is also a relationship between the value of our assets and annual flow of factor payments.

There are two competing views of how best to measure a person's ability to pay taxes. One view is generally associated with the names of Schanz, Haig and Simons (referred to as S-H-S combine). The other view is linked to the names of Hobbes, Fisher and Kaldor (referred to as H-F-K combine). The supporters of these two combines claim that their own measure of ability to pay principle is equitable, efficient and simple to administer.

History of Income Tax

Like many other taxes, the income tax too was introduced as a war-time tax. For the first time, it was introduced in Great Britain during the Napoleonic wars. It had the precedents of many interesting experiments. Poll taxes were introduced in the 14th century. There were other unfamiliar taxes such as 'duties on silver plates' (1765), 'window tax' (1769), 'male servants tax' (1777), 'female servants' (1778), 'inhabited house duties' (1778), 'sporting licenses and game keepers' (1779), etc. Pitt, the Young, was prime minister of Great Britain when the

Napoleonic wars broke out. He first introduced bizarre taxes such as 'duties on hair powder' (1795), 'on dogs' (1796), and 'clocks and watches' (1798). He introduced income tax in the year 1799. Income up to £60 was exempted and the tax was imposed at 10 per cent flat. Each taxpayer was required to file a return of his income under nineteen different heads. It was, however, withdrawn in the year 1816. But, it was re-imposed by Peel and finally, it was Gladstone who declared income tax as "an engine of gigantic power for great national purposes". By 1860, the Crimean War had supervened (1854-56) and Gladstone had no choice but to re-impose income tax indefinitely.

The history of income tax in India is nearly 150-year old. It was introduced as a temporary measure in 1860 to meet the financial stringency arising out of the mutiny of 1857. From 1860 to 1866, the income tax law of 1860 had an uneasy existence in as much as it was abolished in one year, reinforced in another, withdrawn again in a subsequent year and then re-imposed again. Between 1860 and 1866, as many as twenty-three acts were passed. The Act of 1886 is regarded as the first systematic legislation. It served the purpose of a forerunner to the subsequent acts. The Income Tax Act of 1961 is currently in force. Taxpayers are classified into six categories, namely, individuals, Hindu Undivided Family, companies, local authorities, firms or partnerships and association of persons. Income from different sources is also classified into six heads namely: salaries, interest on securities, income from property, profits or gains from business or profession, capital gains and income from other sources.

Definition of Income

The term income is very broad; it practically covers all that comes in. The Chart 5.1 depicts different sources of income.

There are different notions of income, such as personal income, disposable income, national income, per capita income, national income at factor cost, net national income, and others, each having its own significance, for example, per capita income is taken as an index of economic growth.

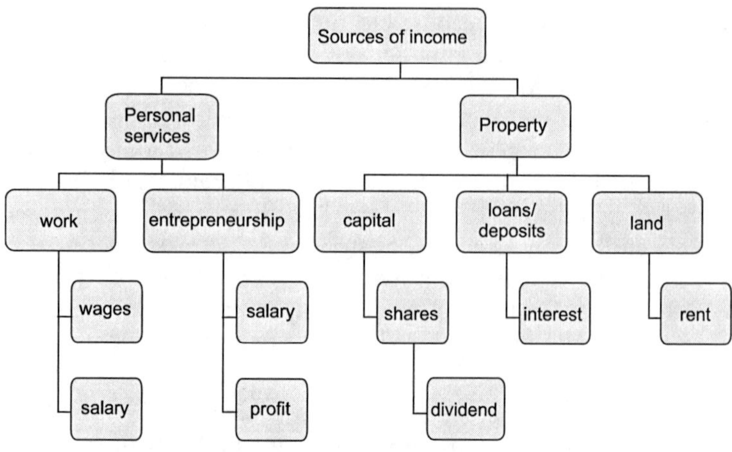

Chart 5.1: Sources of Income

For the purpose of taxation, income must be something clearly definable, quantitatively observable and objectively measurable. Objectivity leads to clarity which makes room for simplicity. Simplicity, largely, leads to a transparent system. Notable contributions in the field of definition of income are those of R.M. Haig, Henry Simons and Nicholas Kaldor. There are a few German contributions which have, unfortunately, received less attention, such as, Hermann, Roscher, A. Held, and Schanz. However, among these the definition as developed by Schanz has received relatively more attention. Modern public finance experts speak of a definition of income as S-H-S combine, i.e., Schanz, Haig and Simons. Musgrave maintains that a vast German literature on definition of income in general and writings of Schanz in particular, have influenced the thinking of Henry Simons.[1]

Professor R.M. Haig's definition of income is considered in theory as most satisfactory.[2] He defines income as the money value of net accretions to economic power between two

1. Musgrave, Richard A., *The Theory of Public Finance*, *op. cit.*, pp. 160-67.
2. Haig, R.M., *The Concept of Income*, Columbia University Press, 1921, especially Chapter 1. See also Nicholas Kaldor's *An Expenditure Tax*, George Allen and Unwin, London, Third Impression, p. 37.

points of time. A large number of authors have acknowledged the comprehensiveness of his definition. This definition incorporates within itself all incomings on accrual basis without regard to the sources. It is immaterial whether the economic power was accrued through employment or business, by holding property or selling it, was it a windfall or a gift from near and dear ones, was regular or irregular or fell in one's lap without effort, was it fluctuating or stable or was it real or nominal?

Even though Haig's definition is very comprehensive yet, in the context of equity criterion, it cannot be fully applied for the purpose of measuring ability to pay. It is absolutely necessary to differently treat different sources of income. For example, labour income and income from property cannot be treated equally. All the above mentioned sources cannot be taxed using personal income tax only. This requires as many taxes as are the sources. One may argue here that while a personal income tax may take care of income from salary, a wealth tax may be imposed on different forms of property. This argument definitely makes a sense but what essentially forgotten is the point that we have to go on adding several such taxes to cover various components of income. The necessity of wealth tax, or for that matter other taxes, is a case against an income tax that this tax by itself is not in a position to achieve goals of equity and redistribution.

The most often quoted definition of income, regarded as a classic one, is that of Henry Simons.[3] He defines income as an algebraic sum of (1) estimating the amount by which the value of a person's store of property rights would have increased, over a period of time, had nothing been consumed, or by (2) estimating the value of the rights which might have been exercised in consumption without altering the value of the store of rights. Personal income, therefore, can be thought of in terms of consumption and accumulation and can be defined as the algebraic sum of an individual's consumption expenses and accumulation during an accounting period. Symbolically:

3. Simons, Henry, *Personal Income Taxation,* Chicago University Press, 1938, p. 128.

$$PY = C + \Delta W$$

where

PY = personal income,

C = consumption,

ΔW = the change in the value of a person's assets over an accounting period.

Raja Chelliah has very ably summarized the accretion principle as under[4]:

1. All earnings including investment income minus cost of earning and depreciation.
2. Net accrued capital gains and imputed value of services or utility of non-business assets owned minus depreciation and cost of maintenance.
3. Imputed value of services rendered by members of household to themselves, and
4. Casual receipts such as lottery, prizes, gifts, bequests, inheritances, etc.

While the above concept provides a theoretically ideal measure of taxpaying capacity, it must be recognized immediately that no real world tax conform to it perfectly. It is really a matter of great surprise that while Simons's definition of income has attracted the attention of economists world-wide, difficulties and ambiguities as explained by Simons himself are rarely mentioned. Simons was careful to say that the definition was not suitable for all purposes and would not without modification be described as satisfactory. Some more obvious difficulties and limitations as explained by Simons himself are:

1. The definition raises an unanswerable question as to where and how a line is to be drawn between what is and what is not an economic activity. If a man raises vegetables in his garden, it seems clearly appropriate to include the value of product in measuring income. Simons refers to Kleinwatcher conundrums who

4. Chelliah, Raja J., "Case for An Expenditure Tax", *Economic and Political Weekly*, January 26, 1980.

suggests that the poorest families might be shown to have substantial income if one went on accounting for services rendered unto themselves.

2. Henry Simons cites another Kleinwatcher conundrum. Here the issue is measurement of incomes of an officer serving with troops and the ADC to the Sovereign. Both receive same nominal pay. But, the latter has a quarter in palaces, food at the royal table, servants, and horses for sports, etc. He accompanies price to the opera and in brief, lives royally at no expense of his own. The problem is clearly hopeless. To include all income in kind is difficult and to leave it is iniquitous.
3. Simons admits another difficulty which is associated with valuation of assets held. This requires regular trading, existence of perfect markets, wide information and sound judgement.
4. Simons acknowledges that there is no rigorous, objective method either of measuring or of allowing for instability in monetary *numeraire*.

Nicholas Kaldor offers his own definition of income which speaks of a real change.[5] Even though Kaldor has not directly contributed to the definition of income, in his survey of the concept of income in economic theory, he provides his comments which contain all the features of a good definition which economists usually favour. He remarks that the ideal definition of income as a measure of taxable capacity, is to be thought of, not as consumption plus actual capital accumulation (*a la* Haig) nor as consumption plus capital excluding windfall (the accountancy ideal) but consumption plus a real capital accumulation, where the term real capital accumulation is to be understood as actual capital accumulation subjected to a double series of corrections: first, for the change in general level of prices (of consumers' goods) and second, for the change in general level of interest rates.

From the definition of Nicholas Kaldor, one gets the impression that:

5. Kaldor, Nicholas, *op. cit.*, pp. 54-78.

1. It is possible to define income in theory.
2. Economically justifiable definition of income should be offered in real terms only.
3. Income can be defined in money terms and its measurement is also possible.
4. Income measured in money terms as an index of ability to pay should be corrected for changes in price level and interest rates.

This fact must be admitted that a test involving a double series of corrections in terms of changes in prices and interest rates is bound to be highly complicated and at the same time, highly arbitrary. Progressive taxation requires that valuation be held at regular intervals. Every year assets either appreciate or depreciate in value. When assets are regularly traded or sold, their value is easily determined. But not all assets are traded regularly and, therefore, a considerable degree of arbitrariness enters into valuation. Experience indicates that valuation is beset with endless and confusing interpretation, costly litigation and, therefore, must be avoided to the extent possible.

The S-H-S combine has resulted in an explanation of income that is popularly referred to as the accretion principle. Economists, for the purpose of taxation regard S-H-S combine as the best definition. But, at the same time, they maintain that in agreeing on an appropriate definition of income, they do not necessarily accept income as an appropriate tax base. They, for one reason or the other, prefer to tax numerous receipts separately but in process, this increases the number of taxes making the system more complicated and confusing.

Income Tax and Equity

As pointed out earlier, the S-H-S principle requires that all accretions to economic power should be included in the tax base. It should be done without regard to the fact that a unit of accretion was realized or not, was it expected or otherwise and so on. When this approach is adhered to, several problems arise inadvertently. Sometimes, they attract the attention of policy-makers and tax administrators; largely they go unnoticed and unattended. Inevitably, at a certain stage in the definition and measurement of income, economists and accountants adopt two conflicting approaches. Economists emphasize accretions and that too in real terms. The accountants, on the other, talk only of realization and that too, in money terms. It is very possible that while computing tax liability of a person, the economists and accountants may arrive at two different conclusions. If income, for the purpose of taxation and as an index of ability to pay, is not measured satisfactorily, then inequitable treatment of taxpayers is a definite possibility. If we wish to have income tax as the main form of direct taxation, the rule of equity requires that income for tax purposes should be so defined as to adequately represent spending power. If the definition of income is defective, then people in similar circumstances would get taxed unequally.

It is now admitted that while it is theoretically possible to define income in a manner to cover all important elements of spending power, in practice, it is not possible to measure many of them satisfactorily. As a result, the measurement of tax base turns out to be misleading creating inequities. Certain problem areas are identified as under:

1. *Realisation versus Accretion*

The S-H-S combine defines income as consumption plus increase in net worth. Increase is measured by comparing net worth valued at market prices at the beginning and end of a period. For example, if a piece of real property rises in value from $100,000 to $200,000, there is then a corresponding increase in net worth. From the viewpoint of accretion principle, it is immaterial whether gains have been realized or not. This conflicts with conventional accounting approach according to which income is recognized only when gains are converted into cash. From economists' viewpoint, increase in net worth should be considered. Accountants maintain that the inclusion of accretions causes high degree of arbitrariness. They, therefore, are in favour of its exclusion. Economists complain that exclusion of an important component of accretion leads to under-taxation.

In order to overcome the problem of taxing unrealized accretions to economic power, two suggestions are usually put forth:

1. Valuation of assets at regular intervals.
2. Imposition of a tax on real assets after demise of taxpayer.

At this juncture, it is worth to recall here that the valuation of assets is beset with numerous difficulties. It requires perfect knowledge of prices and market conditions. It is our experience that markets are known for asymmetric information. The possibilities of undervaluation of assets cannot be ruled out. The latter proposition of taxing assets after demise of taxpayer may be criticized on the following grounds:

1. It leads to the postponement of tax payment.
2. It narrows the existing base.
3. It favours taxpayer to enjoy unrealized accretions, a sense of well-being and security until his death without paying any tax.
4. Any tax after the death of a taxpayer might cause great hardship to his heirs notwithstanding the net loss following his death.

The danger of unequal treatment looms large. Include unrealized gains and be ready for arbitrariness; exclude them and be ready for impairing equity. A comprise between economists and accounts is only a distant possibility.

2. *Income in Money Terms and Income in Real Terms*

From economic viewpoint, it is necessary that accretions as an index of ability should be measured in real terms. The value of accretions at the end of a period must be deflated in order to determine a real change in value. This is being advocated on two grounds. First, on account of inflation accretions are just nominal. Secondly, it is necessary to work out depreciation. Our task is to determine an appropriate price index for pointing out real appreciation and depreciation. As a matter of principle all assets and liabilities should be adjusted for changes in price level and accretions need be measured only in real terms. Economists, however, maintain that it is hardly possible to carry out these adjustments except in cases such as inventory valuation. In view of this equity is impaired by piecemeal adjustments to allow for price-level changes in selected parts of the system.

3. *Fluctuating versus Stable Income*

We know that contributions to spending power are numerous. These may be stable or fluctuating. By nature the fluctuating contributions are essentially different from stable contributions and, therefore, these should be treated separately. Applying a single yardstick of measurement to these accruals appears to be unrealistic. Unfortunately, under the accretion principle, these two are not treated differently. From accretion viewpoint, it is immaterial whether income is received at regular or irregular intervals. Here a taxpayer who often receives large fluctuating income has to pay more tax than a recipient of stable income even though the taxpayer has less control over the source and timing of accretion. "This violates the principle of equal treatment. There is no reason as to why the index of equality should be defined in terms of income received over one year period rather than over several years. Indeed a good case could be made in terms of defining the index of equality in terms of lifetime income."[6]

If tax rates were proportional, there would not have been a serious problem of equity even if income was received at irregular intervals. Progressive taxation, however, is a rule of the day and it requires averaging a taxpayer's volatile income. In this case, yearly assessment goes against the interest of taxpayer because progressive taxation of fluctuating income is naturally severe. It is also agreed that averaging is complicated and in times of rapidly rising prices, averaging devices become meaningless. Averaging of income at short intervals makes the work of computation considerably difficult.

---

6. Musgrave, Richard A., *op. cit.*, p. 170.

4. *Imputed Income*

Benefits from services and income in-kind are also important forms of accretions to economic power. Not all income is obtained through market transaction and in-cash. Food grown and consumed of home farm, rent saved by owner occupancy, services rendered by housewives, *et al.*, are no less important in value than other accretions. A line, therefore, should necessarily be drawn as to what is and what is not an accretion for tax purposes. Experience, however, has proved that this line, as and when drawn, would be highly arbitrary.

It may be noted here that the poorer classes do many jobs on their own as against the rich sections of society who have to pay for many services. Poor people, therefore, are said to have higher imputed income and thereby are required to pay high taxes. Thus, a paradoxical situation is created. Further, not only benefits flowing from self-services need to be included but a suitable allowance should also be made for headaches, backaches and sleepless nights in the course of various types of jobs. Failure to compute imputed income makes an important component of accretion to escape tax free.

From the foregoing examination of the accretion principle, it is observed that at the end of each accruing component, its picture is not clear. Many difficulties arise and paradoxes abound in number. In our efforts to counter these, some highly arbitrary adjustments have to be made at the cost of an equitable and just system of taxation.

Following Musgrave, Raja Chelliah has also pointed out some distinct difficulties in defining and measuring the concept of income for tax purposes[7]:

1. There is accrual in the form of a share in undistributed profits of companies. Even though suggestions have been made for the full integration of corporation tax and individual income tax, under which the share in undistributed profits of corporation could be taxed in the hands of respective shareholders, it is widely

7. Chelliah, Raja J., *op. cit.*

agreed that the integration of two taxes leads to insuperable difficulties.

2. There is the accrual of capital gains on assets owned. Since several of those assets such as unquoted stock and physical assets of proprietary business are not traded continually, it is difficult to compute their market value from year to year. Moreover, taxation of net capital gains on an accrual basis is likely to lead to hardship, i.e., liquidity problems for taxpayers. Hence, capital gains can in practice be taxed only on realization basis. This leads to low tax burden on some individuals. Moreover, the taxation of realized capital gains under progressive taxation requires that gains be averaged over a period of years to avoid inequity. Finally there arises often the problem of separating out real capital gains from nominal increases in monetary value through inflation.
3. There are items of income in-kind, in the form of utility flowing from non-business assets owned by taxpayers and in the form of services rendered unto themselves by members of a family. Imputation of proper values to these is almost impossible.
4. In case of businesses, economic depreciation has to be estimated in order to derive true income. As is well known, this is a Herculean task even if there is no inflation in the general price level.

Two questions are, thus, asked oftenly:

1. What is wrong if some accretions to economic power are excluded?
2. What if some components of accretions to economic power receive differential treatment?

These questions necessitate a thorough examination of aftermath of non-exclusion and or differential treatment of a few components of accretions. It is visualized that:

1. The less exclusive tax base, higher has to be the rate of a tax to obtain a given sum of revenue.

2. Inequity intensifies with progression in the scale of taxation.
3. Non-inclusion of certain forms of accretion or separate and moderate taxation of still others favour rich taxpayers.

Thus, a privileged class of taxpayers manages to reduce tax burden at the cost of loss of revenue to the national exchequer. This imposes high marginal tax burden on those who, unlike their privileged brethren, are not in a position to reduce their tax burden.

In the light of observations and questions raised above, it appears that equitable income taxation is a remote hope. The present system is perceived to be inequitable as it makes individuals and families in equal positions to pay different amounts of tax. The presence of inflation has caused a systematic overstatement of income and pushed more and more taxpayers into high income brackets for no fault of their own. At the same time, no satisfactory provisions are available in the system to differentiate nominal accretions from real accretions. Wages, commissions, profits and salaries are fully taxed but fringe benefits are not fully taxed. People are troubled by stories of individuals and corporations which pay no or a little tax. The system has become so complicated that almost all taxpayers seek experts' advice. Complexities lead to excessive tax planning and rearranging of personal and business affairs for tax minimizing purposes. High marginal rates create a drag on economic growth by penalizing innovation, efficiency, hard work, saving and investment and more by diverting people's attention towards tax avoidance.

The Root Cause

The root cause of this state of affairs lies in the inability of experts to suitably define and properly measure the very basis of taxation, i.e., income! It is admitted that the income tax theorists have been less successful in explaining why accretions should be the best index of equity; instead its supposed superiority has been taken for granted. In several countries where income tax occupies a prime position, income for tax purposes is not defined, simply various sources are enumerated. For example, in case of India, the Income Tax Act enumerates different sources of income and prescribes the method of computing income under six heads; income as such is not defined. Thus, in the absence of (i) a precise definition of income and (ii) universal measurement of different constituents of income, the tax computation gets more confusing and complicated. Here, certain pertinent questions cannot be avoided. These are:

1. Is income a most satisfactory overall criterion to take as the basis for taxation?
2. Is income most satisfactory measure of ability to pay?
3. Is the income tax as found in practice in several countries equitable and just?
4. Has not inflation accentuated equity related problems?
5. Should a refuge be taken in the alternative index of ability to pay?

Basis for Taxation: Consumption

6

Objective: To examine suitability of consumption base.
Organization: historical development; Fisher's contribution; Kaldor's pioneering efforts; post-Kaldor developments; defining consumption; equity criterion; arguments against, hybrid base.

The idea that personal expenditure, reflecting different levels of consumption expenditure, may also be a base for direct taxation has coincided with income base ever since it was first time introduced in Great Britain in 1799. Economists of repute have developed a powerful and appealing case for an expenditure tax. Kaldor writes: "There can be a few ideas in the field of economics which are so revolutionary in their implications and yet can look back on so respectable an ancestry."[1]

Historical Development of the Concept

It was nearly three hundred years ago that the idea of taxing expenditure was first mooted by Thomas Hobbes in his much quoted book *Leviathan*. His statement is usually put in the first line of defence of an expenditure tax. He remarks: "For what reason is there that he which laboureth much and sparing the fruits of his labour consumeth little should be more charged than he that living idly getteth little and spendeth all

1. Kaldor, Nicholas, *op. cit.*, p. 11.

he gets. Seeing that one hath no more protection from the common wealth than the other? But when the impositions are layed upon those things which men consume, every man payeth actually for what he useth; nor is the common wealth defrauded by luxurious waste of private men."

The Hobessian statement is an attempt in the direction of demonstrating virtue of saving over consumption. This also reflects the then prevailing strand of thinking where saving was favoured for capital formation. Similarly, Hobbes mention of luxurious waste requires some more attention. Generally, rich are found indulging in conspicuous consumption which does not serve any development purpose. In this way, resources are not made available for their more productive deployment. At the same time, the consumption pattern of others, especially of middle income class, is adversely affected through the "demonstration effect". When more resources are wasted in an unwanted manner, less tends to be the chances of productive utilization, capital formation and thereby economic growth.

After Hobbes, the case for an expenditure tax was picked up by J.S. Mill who pleaded for the exemption of savings at length on several occasions especially before the *Select Committee on Income and Property Taxes of 1861*. He challenged justness ascribed to income tax declaring that no income tax is really just from which savings are not exempt and no income tax ought to be voted without that provision. He maintains that unless savings are exempt from the income tax, the contributors are taxed twice. For saved and invested (and generally speaking all savings are invested) it pays income tax on the interest or profit which it brings notwithstanding that it has already been taxed on the principal. To tax the sum invested and afterwards tax also the proceeds of investment is to tax the same portion of income twice over.

Mill's argument of double taxation of savings has led to the birth of one of the classical debates in economics. Mill was supported, among others, by Marshall and Pigou from England, Fisher from United States and Eianudi from Italy. Fisher's analogy of fruit and tree is very famous. When a tree is taxed, fruits should be ignored and when fruits are taxed, the tree should be ignored. Taxing both fruits and tree has no economic sense. Recent studies also support Mill's contention. These have pointed out that a serious drawback of an accretion base is that it leads to what is time and again called as "double taxation of saving".

The case for an expenditure tax as developed by Mill does not go beyond the debate of double taxation. After Mill, Alfred Marshall maintained that a graduated expenditure tax is superior to all other forms of direct taxes. He, however, described it as a *Utopian goal.* Pigou too developed the case for an expenditure tax on the line of Mill and Marshall. He writes: "A general income tax as understood in England can be shown to differentiate against investment, i.e., the saving use of income and so differentiates in favour of rival."[2] Pigou explains his case more convincingly than Mill and Marshall. According to Pigou, an income tax hits equally at the income which is saved and the income which is spent. Although this appears real in the first instance, it is, however, illusory. An income tax discriminates against savings by hitting the principal as well as the yield. It strikes at a rate of x per cent at that part of income which is spend at this rate. But if £100 is saved, it removes £x at that moment and thereafter, removes also parts of fruits yielded by it. In his evidence before the *Colwyn Committee on National Debt and Taxation* (1927), Pigou referred to the impossibility of preventing dishonest citizens making a practice of saving in one year, thus, escaping taxation and secretly selling out and spending their savings in the next year. Keynes too in his own evidence before the said Committee maintained that while an expenditure tax is "perhaps theoretically sound, it is practically impossible".

A close study of the ideas of Mill, Marshall and Pigou reveals certain common features in their writings:

1. These authors laid a heavy emphasis on the double taxation of savings, thus, restricting the case for an expenditure tax.

---

2. Pigou, A.C., *A Study in Public Finance,* 3rd Edition, MacMillan & Co., 1949, pp. 117-18.

2. They were not aware or probably did not foresee the equity problems involved in defining and measuring the concept of income as used for tax purposes. In a sense, they were right in not raising this issue because inequities do not arise much when a proportional rate is in vogue.
3. All these authors were highly doubtful about the administrative feasibility of an expenditure tax.

Contribution of Fisher

Irving Fisher is regarded as the sufferer for a cause. He is at the very front among the American exponents of the expenditure tax, known there as spendings tax. He provided definition of consumption; demonstrated the possibility of an indirect computation of chargeable expenditure and gave a mathematical proof of double taxation of savings. Of his innumerable writings, the most notable ones are *Nature and Scope of Capital and Income* (1906), *Income in Theory and Income Taxation in Practice* (1937), *Double Taxation of Savings* (1939) and *Constructive Income Taxation* (1942). Unfortunately, the students of economics know about Fisher in the context of quantity theory of money and preparation of index numbers. Thus, they do no justice to Fisher, who almost single handedly took up the cause of an expenditure tax in United States.

Prior to Fisher, economists were under the impression that it was not possible to monitor consumption expenditure and they, therefore, were doubtful about the administrative feasibility of an expenditure tax. Fisher maintains that it is not necessary to track a taxpayer in his spending spree dollar by dollar. The same could be monitored indirectly. Kaldor admits: "The idea that a graduated tax based on personal expenditure may be administratively feasible proposition impressed itself on my mind and stood me in good stead when I came to deal with problem of taxation fifteen years later."[3] Fisher's major work *Constructive Income Taxation* was published in 1942 but suffered oblivion in the mid-war frenzy of three continents.

3. Kaldor, Nicholas, *op. cit.*, footnote, p. 12.

Right from the days of Mill, the case for an expenditure tax has come to be invariably associated with the double taxation of savings. In this field too, the contribution of Fisher is seminal for he provided a mathematical proof of double taxation. The argument probably the most basic argument as well as most neglected. For this argument, we need not depend upon authority. There is a mathematical proof, the proof that if savings are taxed as income and again income from these savings is also taxed, there will be subtle form of double taxation.[4]

The scholarly writings of Fisher and his painstaking efforts to popularize an expenditure tax did not receive due attention. The reasons appear to be a combination of circumstances. During the Second War and in the postwar period, Friedman, Tobin and Poole pleaded for an expenditure tax as an anti-inflationary measure.[5]

Kaldor's Pioneering Efforts

Any discussion on expenditure tax must revert to the pioneering contributions of Nicholas Kaldor. In fact, the two have become synonyms. Both his protagonists and antagonists hold him in high regard. His book *An Expenditure Tax* (1955) received world-wide attention for a masterly presentation of the case for a tax which was regarded as the best in theory but difficult to administer in practice. He revived the idea of taxing personal consumption expenditure by bringing to the notice of fellow economists, and public as well, the problems which arise from a defective definition and measurement of income. He also pointed out inequities and inefficiencies which arise from having a defective income tax in practice.

Before Fisher and Kaldor, the case for an expenditure tax was irretrievably confined to double taxation of savings. Kaldor based his case on at least three major arguments all of which were departures from those of his predecessors.

4. Fisher, Irving, "Double Taxation of Savings", *American Economic Review*, Vol. 29, 1939, pp. 17-33.
5. For further details one may refer to Sayed Afzal Peerzade's *Expenditure Tax in India*, Anmol Publications, New Delhi, 1990.

Although Kaldor is satisfied with the traditional justification of taxation of income, it appears that his discontent is primarily with concept of income as used in the matters of taxation. It is on this ground that the whole case for an expenditure tax is developed. He asks: "Is income the most satisfactory overall criterion to take as the basis for such taxation?"

It is a matter of great surprise that a comparatively less attention is paid to examine a centrally important question as mentioned above. This is because of the fact that after being in operation for more than two hundred years, income tax came to be regarded as the most acceptable explanation of ability to pay. However, Kaldor asserts that not only our existing definition of income for tax purposes is an extremely defective measure of taxable capacity but any conceivable alternative definition of income is also bound to be defective in varying degrees even when taken in conjunction with supplementary taxes on wealth. A few of his major arguments in favour of an expenditure tax are as under:

1. There is involved an arbitrariness in the measurement of income. This arises on account of the fact that the sources of spending power are numerous and these cannot be reduced to a common denominator except on some highly arbitrary basis.
2. The prevailing concept of income is far different from the one ideally defined. On one hand, the base in practice includes some forms, on the other it excludes a few others. A few are taxed at preferential rates and others at ordinary rates resulting in numerous capricious inequities.
3. Presently, some forms of savings are exempt; some forms are taxed at preferential rates and still others are charged fully. In general, we make no attempt to charge dissaving. If saving is economically desirable, so also is the prevention of dissaving. An expenditure tax is doubly superior to an income tax as it simultaneously encourages saving and discourages dissaving.

4. An expenditure tax is superior to even a comprehensive income tax (CIT). This is because of the fact that even though CIT by definition covers all types of accretion, the problem of reducing them to a common unit of spending power remains. Here an expenditure tax has an advantage in the sense that it is no longer necessary to enquire into the nature of accruals. For example, if capital gains are spent to the extent that they are actually realized, there is no need to inquire how far they were real or fictitious. Similarly, accruals (flow) from net worth (stock) get taxed when spent, doing away with the need of a periodic valuation of assets owned.

In a Conference organized by the Brookings Institution in 1978 at Washington D.C., Kaldor renewed his earlier claim. "I, therefore, come down in favour of an expenditure tax principle not because the existing system of income taxation is defective but because the basic limitations of income concept make it impossible to implement the Haig-Simons formulation, no matter how the tax laws are framed."[6] He further maintained that the test of an expenditure tax is not to see that savings are exempted but dissavings are charged. It is a charge on dissavings, and not exemption of savings, that distinguishes an expenditure tax from an income tax.

Post Kaldor Developments

In early 1960s, following the recommendations of Kaldor, the expenditure tax was introduced in India and Sri Lanka. It, however, had a very bitter experience. A very bright idea was put to practice at wrong time and at wrong places. Nevertheless, the academic interest in expenditure tax continues to remain unfazed. In late seventies and early eighties of previous centuries, several reports and studies have come out in favour of an expenditure tax. Among them, the most notable are *Blueprints for Basic Tax Reform* (U.S.), *Meade Committee Report* (U.K.) and *Lodin Commission Report* (Sweden) *Understanding Tax Reform: A Guide to*

6. Pechman, Joseph, *What Should Be Taxed: Income or Expenditure?* Brookings Institution, Washington D.C., 1980, p. 153.

21st Century Alternatives, (AICPA-US). In addition to these, numerous scholars all over the world have made several sterling contributions. Their findings and recommendations can be summarized as under:

1. An expenditure tax stimulates savings which facilitate necessary supply of productive capital.
2. It treats all sources of income alike and makes the practice of conversion of one form of income into another less attractive.
3. There is no need for inflation indexation as the expenditure is always in money terms and at current prices.
4. It has all the potential of an effective counter-cyclical tool.

To sum up, it can be said that the future of an expenditure tax is most bright now for the specific reason that the income tax suffers from schizophrenia. There are so many deductions and exemptions that one is at loss to regard the present income tax as a straight accretion-based levy. In fact, it neither conforms to pure accretion ideal nor consumption ideal. It is now a hybrid of the two, resembling to accretion base in some respects and consumption base in other.

Defining Consumption

It is pointed out in the previous pages that one of the major requirements of a good definition, particularly in the matters of taxation, is clarity. This in turn leads to an objective measurement of tax base. It is possible only when clear notions are established as to what does and what does not constitute a component of a particular tax base. In this respect, even the pioneers in the definition of income have clearly expressed their reservations. In fact, income as a base is not defined; simply its sources are enumerated for tax purposes. The basic issue to examine here is amenability of concept of consumption to definition. And when defined, is it superior to income definition as a better measure of taxable capacity?

Consumption is defined in several ways. One of the popular notion is that it a difference between income and savings. Fisher defines consumption as "consisting of those particular uses or services which give direct satisfaction to the user, that is, satisfaction without intervention of further productive process".[7] There are two important points in Fisher's definition. First, consumption in the broadest sense is a sense of satisfaction from the use of goods and services. Here we can visualize two types of consumption: (1) objective consumption, and (2) subjective consumption. Objective consumption is expressed and measured in terms of prices paid for the purchase of goods and services. Now we introduce here an element of cash flow. As against this, it is not possible to express and measure subjective consumption such as star-gazing, bird watching, reading, long morning walks and so on. In the interest of a precise definition and measurement of consumption, it is better to exclude subjective consumption. No payment is made and, therefore, the value of consumption is not reckoned.

Secondly, according to the definition as above, consumption does not result in the intervention of further productive process. Much before Fisher saving was regarded as virtue and consumption a vice. No doubt even today, saving is virtue but consumption is not a vice. Consumption is the ultimate aim of every economic activity. Goods and services do not serve any purpose unless consumed. When goods and services are purchased, directly or indirectly, demand is generated. Consumption in no way restricts economic activity on the contrary it stimulates the same.

Using symbols, the consumption base is normally expressed as:

$$C = R + rW - \Delta W$$

where:

C = consumption

R = non-wealth receipts

rW = rate of return on wealth

ΔW = change in the value of assets.

7. Fisher, Irving, *Constructive Income Taxation,* Harper Bros., 1942, p. 25.

Consumption may be defined to mean a quantitative withdrawal from the common pool. Quantitative withdrawals are given importance because a quantitative assessment is necessary for an objective measurement of the tax base. These are to be exempted up to a certain level and any withdrawal over and above are held taxable. However, not all withdrawals are for consumption alone. Any amount of expenditure for business purpose goes untaxed. It is left to the taxpayer to prove that his expenditure is for the business purpose, otherwise expenditure is taxed as ordinary consumption expenditure.

Consumption is also defined to mean the exercise of economic power. Economic power is exercised only when it is accrued and realized. It is immaterial to probe whether the economic power exercised is real or nominal; earned or unearned; regular or irregular; fluctuating or stable; expected or unexpected and so on. This power gets expressed in money terms. An intelligent taxpayer, in order to minimize his tax liability, tries to "even out" his expenditure, whatever is the source contributing to expenditure. The following Chart 6.1 depicts how different sources of accretions can be reduced to finance consumption expenditure on a cash flow basis.

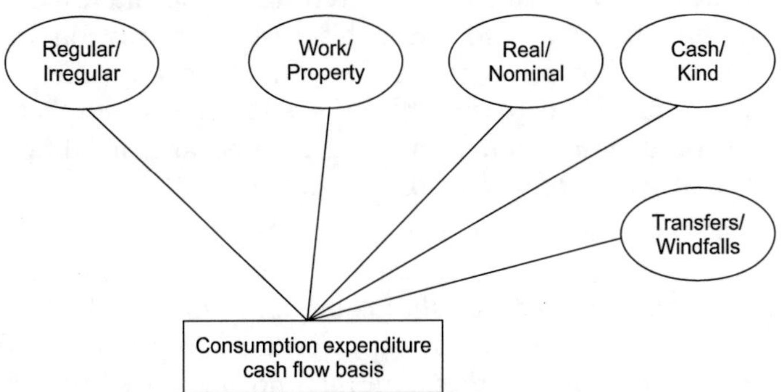

Chart 6.1: Consumption on Cash Flow Basis

Thus, from the viewpoint of definition, the consumption base is a superior choice. It amicably resolves complex problems pertaining to measurement of accretions to economic power. These are not treated differently simply because sources vary. It is equitable because all individuals are taxed according to their respective withdrawals. By definition, the consumption base excludes savings and thereby it avoids double taxation and discriminatory treatment of different forms of savings. As expenditure is always expressed at current prices, the inflation adjustment is easy and simple than under income-based taxation.

Expenditure Tax and Equity

The early advocates of an expenditure tax such as Mill, Marshall, Pigou and Fisher emphasized only the double taxation of savings. They favoured an expenditure tax on the ground that here the double taxation is avoided. Thus, its case came to be associated invariably with the exclusion of savings. Very recently too, a good number of scholars and reports of committees have supported the contention of the early advocates of an expenditure tax that savings are taxed twice under the income tax regime.

No justice is done to the cause of an expenditure tax when its case is kept confined only to the issue of double taxation. The case, however, does not depend only on double taxation but, more importantly it rests solidly on equity argument. It is mainly Kaldor who not only revived academic interest in an expenditure tax but also based his case primarily on more fundamental shortcomings in the concept of income as a measure of taxable capacity. It is now widely perceived that the process of defining and measuring income and its different constituents is full of intractable difficulties.

It is now left to examine whether the definition of consumption satisfies equity criterion? As pointed out earlier, no definition of income satisfies equity criterion for the reason that all accretions to economic power are either not included fully or when included, these are then not measured properly. As against this, the definition of consumption satisfies equity criterion for the reason that all accruals are treated on cash flow basis. A tax is not imposed simply because there is an accrual.

A possible objection to the blanket exclusion of savings or for that matter all accretions unless otherwise spent is that it is beneficial to rich. And, therefore, under an expenditure tax regime, they are unduly benefited. This allegation on equity grounds is valid only when the tax is collected at a proportional rate. The force of this argument is lost when tax rate is made inverse to the marginal propensity to consume.

The expenditure tax does not treat cash balance as savings. A holder of large cash balance suffers on three counts: first, the idle cash balance is not considered as savings and, therefore, it is included in total receipts. Secondly, it is a barren asset and earns nothing. If invested it would have earned anything more than zero. Finally, with inflation as rule of the day, cash balance rapidly depreciates in value. This brings home the point that the rich have to record whatever amount they save, if at all they want to claim a tax deduction. In this way, it is easy to detect taxable expenditure indirectly and apply a progressive rate.

Taxpayers withdraw from and contribute to common pool according to their respective abilities. If this proposition is established, it is then claimed that an expenditure tax is qualitatively more equitable because persons are taxed according to their respective withdrawals. An application of this yardstick reduces the chances of mis-measurement of ability to pay. Inequity mainly arise because of our failure to measure base properly and tax accordingly.

On equity ground, an expenditure tax is a better choice as compared to an accretion type income tax and the income tax of most comprehensive kind. Kaldor asserts that no definition of income which is plausible enough for the purpose of tax assessment can measure taxable capacity.[8] Accruals from various sources cannot be reduced to a common unit of income on any objective criterion. But, each individual performs this operation for himself when, in the light of all his present circumstances and future prospects, he decides on a scale of his personal living expenses. Thus, a tax based on actual spending

8. Kaldor, Nicholas, *op. cit.*, p. 47.

rates each individual's capacity according to the yardstick which he applies to himself.

A great merit of choosing consumption base is that it amicably resolves equity problems arising out of the non-comparability of work income and property income, temporary income and permanent sources of income, regular and irregular income and genuine and fictitious income. These are all treated on cash-flow basis. If contributions to the spending power were a few, if there were proportional taxation, if all incomes were received in cash and if there were no inflation, equity would not have been a major problem even in case of income-base.

Capital gains and for that matter all sorts of appreciations are considered as income even in case of an expenditure tax. But simply their inclusion does not qualify them for taxation. These are taxed only when spent. Currently, under income tax, treatment of capital gains is a key problem. For administrative reasons, capital gains are not taxed on accrual basis and as a result, many wealthy persons and organizations are able to postpone their tax payments indefinitely and reduce their tax liability by converting income into capital gains. Thus, persons capable of converting income into capital are differently treated from those who are not. This problem, however, does not arise when taxation is based upon consumption and any type of accrual is taxed on cash flow basis.

There are a number of arguments for a separate taxation of capital gains and non-inclusion of appreciation. The point here is not their inclusion or separate taxation but conversion of highly taxed ordinary income into lightly taxed capital gains. This has helped wealthy taxpayers to reduce their tax liabilities. They are, thus, unequally taxed. They also maintain comfortable living standard and finance the same by dissavings. The practice of tax shelters combined with separate lower taxation of capital gains has severely impaired equity criterion. In fact, many such devices for reducing income tax liabilities are available and attractive only to the taxpayers with substantial amounts of wealth.

As pointed out earlier, a problem area in income taxation is that of unrealized yet accrued gains. From equity viewpoint, it is immaterial whether gains are realized or not. But, the present tax treatment, following the accounting principle, takes into consideration only realized gains. But, the system as such offers a number of possibilities where realization itself could be postponed. Such of the taxpayers, mainly the owners of capital, who are able to adapt their behaviour to these weaknesses, have managed to reduce their tax burden at the cost of equity principle. Under an expenditure tax, these problems disappear because "if capital gains are taxed to the extent they are spent, there is no need to inquire into how far they are fictitious; it is left to the individual recipient of these gains to sort these things out for himself, in deciding how far he is justified in treating them as spendable gains".[9]

Under the consumption base, another major source which contributes to the realization of equity principle is the fairness involved in the tax treatment of savings. This tax by virtue of its definition excludes all forms of savings and avoids their double taxation. There is no question of partial treatment of different forms of savings.

Individuals and families are known to maintain a stable expenditure pattern. The national income studies conducted by Simon Kuznets, Milton Friedman and Franco Modigliani suggest that average propensity to consume remain stable. Spending decisions at individual and family levels are not governed by current earnings alone but also by previously accumulated balances and future expectations. Stability in consumption minimizes difficulties associated with the taxation of fluctuating and irregular income receipts.

At present, governments all over the world use a number of direct and indirect taxes to mobilize resources and to achieve certain fiscal goals. The use of multiple taxes is an indictment of an income tax that it is iniquitous, unfair and unjust. Not long back, Henry Simons remarked that the income tax is not a tax upon income but a tax upon persons according to their respective incomes.[10] The objective of tax policy must be

9. Kaldor, Nicholas, *op. cit.*, pp. 47-48.
10. Simons, Henry, *op. cit.*, p. 128.

fairness among persons, not fairness among kinds of income receipts (whatever that might be construed to mean). It is possible only under an expenditure tax to do away with a system of differential treatment of different forms of income. Here these come under a single umbrella of cash flow. It seems better to leave individuals free to decide their spending scales and get taxed accordingly.

Arguments Against

There are a few arguments against an expenditure tax which maintain that this tax is not free from loopholes which damage equity criterion. It is alleged that rich taxpayers are favoured as they save more and spend less *vis-à-vis* middle and low income groups. This allegation, however, holds good only when proportionate rate is used. In the area of personal taxation, there is no possibility of applying proportionate rate. Progressive taxation of spending by rich removes doubts regarding under taxation of those who save more and spend less.

An interesting situation arises when it is contended that accumulated savings go on increasing from one generation to the other. Since money begets money, the accumulated balances go on multiplying in a geometric progression. In many cases, wealth is not spent by later generations, but, indeed, added from generation to generation. An expenditure tax never taxes such growing accumulations. This allegation against an expenditure tax holds good only when the issue of accumulated balances is examined in isolation and independent of other supplementary taxes. The fact, however, is that nowhere do we find a system where only one tax is administered. In fact, a favoured one is a system where there are a few taxes, if not many. There is nothing wrong if an expenditure tax is supported by a wealth tax and an accession tax or an estate duty on policy grounds.

Another criticism of an expenditure tax is based on the ground that large families are highly taxed than small families. Problems aggravate when old cohorts live by withdrawing from the previously accumulated balances. In defense of an expenditure tax, it can be said that in designing any direct personal tax, let alone an expenditure tax, the taxpaying unit, size of family, expenditure timings, etc., are all carefully considered.

The argument that there is no double taxation of savings has also run parallel. Richard Musgrave, Kahn, Goode, *et al.*, comment that the term double taxation of savings is pejorative and should be deleted from the vocabulary of tax debate. Chelliah observes that an income tax does not tax savings but income from savings. Further, an expenditure tax is not neutral between consumption and saving. This is quite natural. The important issue to decide is: What should be favoured? Addition to the stock or its depletion? The golden principle indeed is "grow rich and help others to grow rich".

Hybridization of Tax Base: Is the Present Base Income or Consumption?

Over the last few years, consequent of tax expenditures [at personal, instrument and institution levels][11], an interesting development has taken place in the field of direct taxation. This is the emergence of a new tax base termed as "hybrid base". In the light of this development, it is necessary to answer three questions: First, what is a hybrid base? Secondly, why are taxpayers lodged in a hybrid base? Finally, what are the revenue implications of a hybrid tax base?

In a number of countries where the personal income tax occupies a central place, income base is gradually shifting towards the consumption base. Sometimes, it is also possible that the government, implicitly recognizing inherent weakness in the accretion base, may deliberately allow such a shift to achieve certain fiscal goals. But, policy considerations apart, if there is any shift, however small it might be, the original base starts losing its purity because some foreign elements from other base enter into it. The base that so emerges is an unimagined combination of the two or more bases. It becomes much difficult to point out which base is in practice? Is it

11. Tax expenditures are discussed separately in Chapter 3 of this book.

income or consumption? It was Andrews who for the first time termed the income base in practice as a hybrid base.[12]

Accretion concept of income has a little normative value and gives a little help in the practice of income base. There are available so many and so varied devices for tax-free accumulation; so large amounts are invested in such devices and so rapidly are these growing that these have damaged purity of accretion base beyond repair.

The Meade Committee Report (1978) has gone a step ahead. After noting a number of allowable deductions, special provisions and other modifications, it maintains that the tax structure has moved from income base towards what is in effect a consumption base. Indeed in some cases, the combined effect of these modifications is overshooting the mark and to move the tax structure beyond consumption base. This indeed is a very interesting observation; it speaks of the possibility of a fourth base, i.e., a "hybrid base", an outcome of the mixture of two diametrically opposed tax bases.

Over a period of time, a number of consumption base elements have made their inroads into the accretion base. The current tax system exempts, subject to certain limits, many forms of savings. A part of interest-income is exempt from taxation when it is saved in certain government approved forms. Subject to certain limits, savings out of the earnings of an employed person which are contributed to an approved pension scheme, including contributions made on his behalf by his employer, are not subject to tax. Subject to certain limits, in the case of a self-employed person, savings for the purchase of an approved retirement annuity are similarly exempt from tax. Savings through premium for life insurance are also tax-exempt. Similarly, in several countries, unrealized capital gains on financial assets are untaxed as are virtually all capital gains on housing. In the same fashion, realized capital gains are taxed preferentially and are free from all taxation at the death of owner.

---

12. Andrews, William D., "A Consumption Type or Cash Flow Personal Income Tax", *Harvard Law Review,* April 1974.

In the light of these considerations, labeling the income tax as accretion-based tax is a serious misnomer; it is more a hybrid between income and consumption taxes. There is no hesitation in arriving at a conclusion that the treatment of a significant portion of savings under the current tax system more closely resembles the consumption ideal than the income ideal.

All these and many other such provisions may be grouped into three broad categories. First, a part of the amount put into favoured savings schemes is tax-deductible. Second, interest-income from certain favoured financial assets is exempt from tax. Third, both the investment and yield qualify for a deduction, subject to certain limits. The first category comes nearer to the traditional feature of an expenditure tax which favours a full exclusion of savings. The second may be dubbed as a "yield exempt" approach. The third is a shining example of a shift in the base beyond consumption. Despite these possibilities, frustration amongst taxpayers is growing day after day that these saving provisions have not really helped the genuine savers who want to save beyond artificial limits.

From the instances cited above, it is clear that the income base is gradually shifting in favour of consumption ideal. The base as existing today was not imagined by the precursors of modern income tax theorists. Unwillingly though, we have to accommodate, in one way or the other, a few expenditure tax features. A hybrid base, however, neither fully satisfies the accretion ideal nor the consumption ideal; in some cases it conforms to the former; in some other cases to the latter and in case of a few others beyond the latter.

Taxpayers are lodged in a hybrid base for the reason that in practice it is not possible to administer a pure accretion-based income tax. Many governments have intentionally restored to a policy of hybridizing tax base in order to see that the accretion ideal forms the base and certain other objectives are also achieved, such as promotion of saving and investment through tax measures, flow of funds into favoured lines and so on. The rapidity at which this "policy fashion" is spreading is an indication of the fact that the accretion ideal has certain practical limitations. The more it is tried to promote saving and investment, the more that the consumption ideal elements make their inroads compelling the income base to shift away from the original and get hybridized. It appears that under the present circumstances, with deep-rooted value judgements, we just cannot avoid hybridization of the income tax base.

Revenue Implications of Hybrid Base

An attempt is made here to study the revenue implications of a hybrid tax base and to find out how these are different from a pure accretion-based income tax. We proceed on the assumption that the income is defined to mean consumption plus savings; windfalls, gifts bequests and other such related transfers are excluded.

In Fig. 6.1, consumption is measured on OX axis and savings on OY axis. The pre-tax budget line is AB. Following the introduction of an accretion-type income tax at proportionate rate, the post-tax budget line in Fig. 6.1 is A_1B_1. It indicates a high tax burden on savings. This is line with the accretion principle that interest income, investment proceeds and other such receipts should be fully included in the tax base as these are accretions to the economic power.

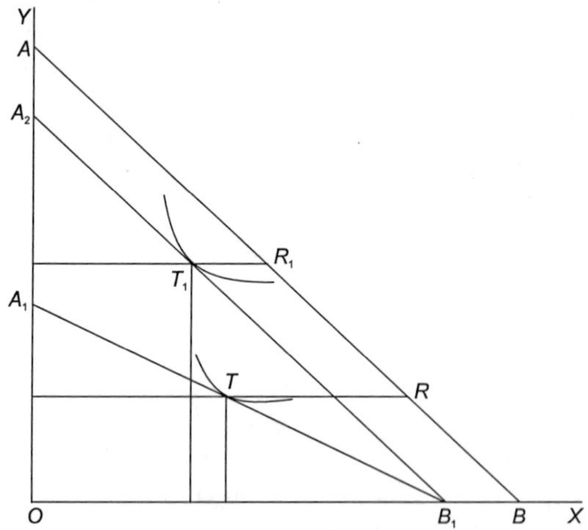

Fig. 6.1: Revenue Implications of Hybrid Tax Base

Now, in line with the broader objectives of fiscal policy government offers reliefs to savings and interest income, etc. This is done on a selective basis thereby introducing clearly the expenditure tax features. Consequently, the new budget line is A_2B_1. It must start from B_1 because the aim of the tax policy is only to promote savings on selective basis and not to tax the present consumption or penalize future consumption. The distance between OA_1 and OA_2 reflects the extent of hybridization. The tax revenue with no savings relief was *TR*. Now, at no point on A_2B_1 it is equal to *TR*.

Thus, the revenue implications of a hybrid base are greatly different from a pure accretion base. The primary function of tax policy should be to raise revenue. But, when it is tied to too many objectives, then the hybridization and consequent shrinkage of the tax base yielding less revenue cannot be avoid.

Economic Effects of Income and Expenditure Taxes

7

Objective: Examination of economic effects of income and expenditure taxes on an individual.

Organization: Introduction; a simple proportional income tax; effects of income tax on spending versus saving; supply of labour; effects of an expenditure tax.

Introduction

Once a justification is developed for raising revenue through different types of taxes, the issue that needs our consideration is the examination of economic effects of taxes on individuals, companies and finally, on the economy. Taxes reduce disposable income; affect the choice between *X* and *Y* types of commodities; consumption and saving; work effort and leisure and different types of investment. Our discussion here is limited only to examine the economic effects of taxes on individuals and their different activities. Various possibilities are examined with the help of simple diagrams, using indifference curve technique.

A tax on personal income of an individual is by far the best known of direct taxes. As pointed out earlier, it is based upon income, i.e., the basis of charge is income. As a base, income is the most popular of three bases namely income, consumption and wealth. It should be noted here that not all the income is considered and computed for tax purposes. A certain portion of income, popularly known as subsistence component of income, is exempted. This is made clear with the help of Fig. 7.1 where years are indicated on OX axis and level of exempt income on OY axis.

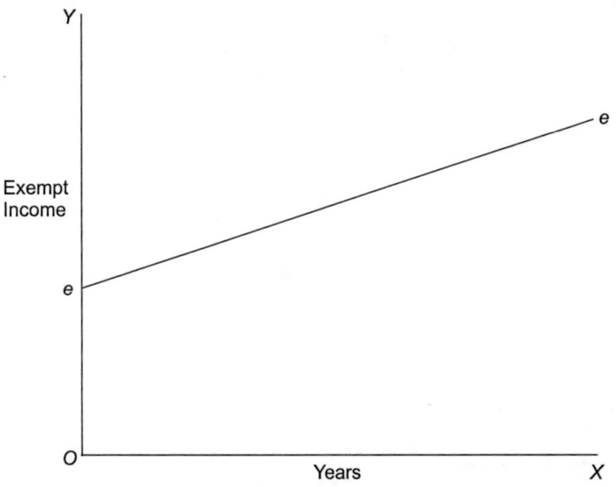

Fig. 7.1: Subsistence and Surplus Components of Income

The curve *ee,* at the height of *Oe* on *OY* axis, expresses the level of exempt income. There is no tax below *ee* but only above *ee*. *Oe* is considered as subsistence component of income whereas any income above *Oe* is held as surplus to which a progressive rate is normally applied. The exemption level of income is revised, may be once in three to four years, to offset a fall in income in real terms on account of inflation. Further, individuals are kept into different income slabs and each slab is tied to a particular rate. More the number of slabs more will be the rates applied. In this way we have a rate structure. The Fig. 7.2 explains possibilities of different rates and slabs administered for income tax purposes.

In Fig. 7.2 level income/consumption is measured on *OX* axis and tax rate on *OY* axis. The curve *mP* is parallel to *OX* axis indicating a proportional tax rate. There is no change in tax rate even if there is a change in the level of income/consumption. This is the reason why a proportional tax is called as a flat rate tax. The curve mnP_1 shows that the rate of tax increases as the income/consumption increase, reflecting certain amount of progression in the rate structure. Within the slab there is no change in the rate, for example, between i and i_1 the tax rate remains same. The rate increases once the taxpayer moves into higher income/consumption slab. The curve mnP_2 indicates a regressive rate structure where the tax rate declines as income/consumption increase.

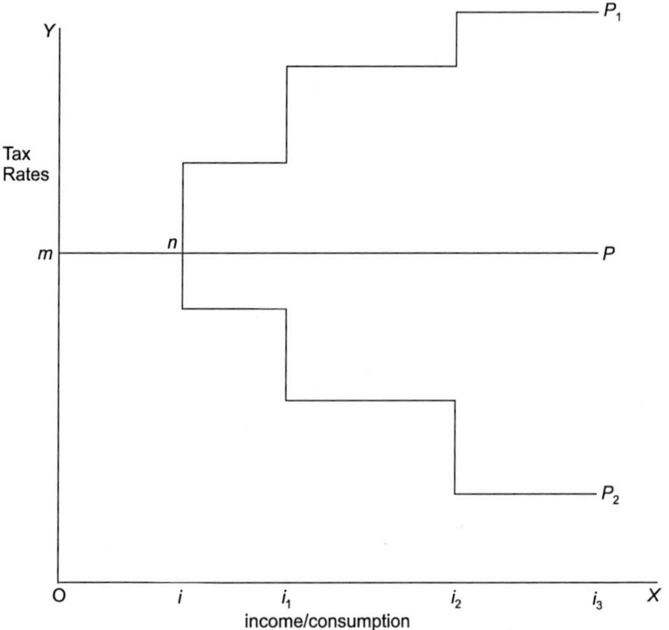

Fig. 7.2: Different Rates and Slabs

A Simple Proportional Income Tax

For the purpose of analytical simplicity, we will not go into the examination of complexities associated with measurement of bases, revision of exemption levels, width of slabs, height of tax rates, etc. We will consider a straightforward case where all such complications are, for the time being, neglected.

Before we proceed ahead, it is necessary that the deliberation of proportional taxation should be justified. The current stream of thinking in the area of tax reform is that the exemption level should be fairly high and that the first tax bracket should be fairly wide. If the first tax bracket is kept wide enough, then for all practical purposes, for a large number of taxpayers and for a long period, the income taxation turns out be proportional one with its own efficiency advantages. Such being the case, theoretically, the consideration of a proportional rate is strong.

Effects, Income Tax on Spending versus Saving

Imposition of a personal income tax does generate economic effects by:

1. Reducing disposable income.
2. Reducing expected income from saving and investment and thereby.
3. Consumption and saving.

Before proceeding further, the effect of a lump sum tax, which is neutral, is examined with the help of Fig. 7.3.

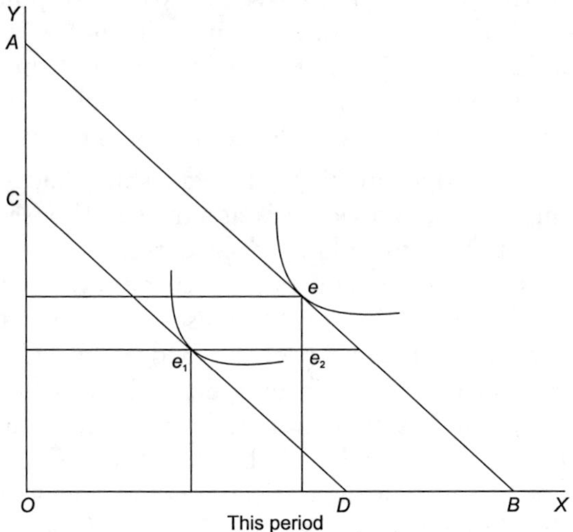

Fig. 7.3: A Neutral Tax

A lump-sum tax is neutral. It does not discriminate between the goods and services available for purchase nor does it affect the choice between consumption in period one and consumption in period two (saving). It only reduces an individual's total income. In Fig. 7.3, *AB* is pretax budget line which is shifted backward, *CD*, on account of imposition of a lump-sum tax. The new budget line *CD* will be positioned below *AB* at a distance where *AC* = *BD*.

Let us now introduce a proportional income tax, dropping the condition of neutrality. Some definite conclusions can be reached about the relative effects of a lump-sum tax and of an income tax. In order to make the comparison strictly one concerned with the form of tax, we must eliminate difference in the total amount of tax levied under two systems. We have to follow the criterion of "equal yield". The comparison is, therefore, between a lump-sum tax and proportional income tax of the equal-yield from the individual in question. Such a comparison is made in the Fig. 7.4.

Following the imposition of a proportional income tax the new budget line shifts backward from *AB* to *CD*. It will not be parallel to *AB*. While point *D* will be close to *B*, point *C* will be at some more distance from *A*. This swing in the budget line is on account of tax on interest receipts which in turn reduces effective net rate of interest received. This swing in the budget line is often referred to as the "double taxation of savings".

The simple proportional income tax shifts budget line to *CD*. On this line the individual is assumed to choose e_1 where *CD* is tangential to the indifference curve IC_1. We have to compare this with lump-sum tax which also yields the same revenue [ee_1 in Fig. 7.3]. Now, because of the "swing-effect" associated with the income tax, the budget line *CD* will be steeper on which the equilibrium point is e_1 where equal-revenue condition is satisfied. This helps us to arrive at the conclusion that the individual is better-off under a lump-sum tax than under a proportional income tax of equal yield, and, secondly the individual saves more [consumes/borrows less] under a lump-sum tax than under a simple proportional income tax.

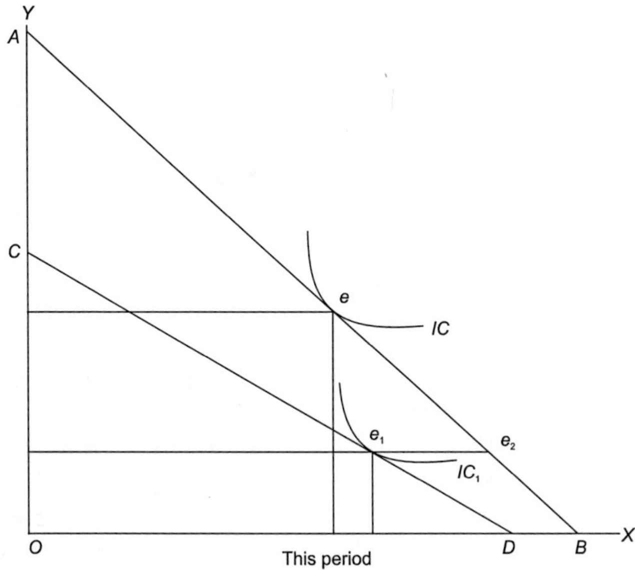

Fig. 7.4: Proportional Income Tax

The above explanation [Fig. 7.4] may be also applied to the income tax treatment of different types of savings which can be, from the viewpoint of taxation, conveniently divided into "most favoured" and "less favoured" types. Some forms of savings are treated favourably by allowing:

1. A full or partial deduction from taxable income.
2. A total exclusion or a partial inclusion of interest income in total taxable income or both.

Let us contemplate that in Fig. 7.4 the tax "favoured savings" are measured on *OX* axis and "less favoured" on *OY* axis. Consequently, the supply of "most favoured" types of savings increases while that of "less favoured" types decreases. This follows the swing in the budget line on account of "double taxation of savings".

Another outcome of above-mentioned treatment, significantly more important in the area of optimal taxation, is that the imposition of a proportional income tax distorts the choice of taxpayers while deciding about:

1. How much to save?
2. Where and in what form to save and invest?

Tax considerations, thus, become more dominating than pure economic and financial considerations.

Effects of Income Tax on Supply of Labour

Economic welfare consists not only of the material income from work but also the psychological benefit individuals received from leisure. Men and women do not live by *GNP* alone. Individuals will maximize their welfare in this respect if they work up to the point where the benefits from a small amount of extra work is just equal to the benefit of taking same amount of time as leisure. Below that level, the marginal benefit from work exceed those from leisure and above that level the reverse is true.

Examining the supply curve of labour is perhaps the simplest way of tackling this issue. If the supply curve of labour is upward sloping like *SS* in the following Fig. 7.5, it follows that an increase in income tax rate will reduce the number of hours worked. This can be seen by imagining the pre-tax net wage rate to be W_1 and the hours worked to be H_1. An increase in income tax reduces the net wage rate to W_2 and the hours of work to H_2.

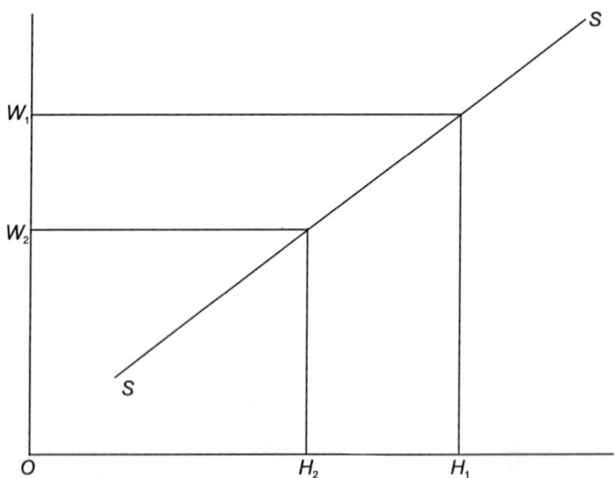

Fig. 7.5: Income Tax and Supply of Labour

However, it is true that in these circumstances, an income tax is a disincentive to work effort, in other circumstances, it may result in more work. Suppose now that the supply curve of labour bends back on itself, as in the following Fig. 7.6. This simply means that if wage rate rise beyond a certain point people will to choose to work less. This may be interpreted as individuals choosing to enjoy part of their increased prosperity in the form of more leisure. Historically, in industrialized countries hours of work have fallen as wage rates have increased and there are empirical evidences to this effect. In these circumstances, a similar increase in income tax will result in more work hours. In Fig. 7.6, a drop in after-tax wage rate from W_3 to W_4 will result in an increase in hours worked from h_3 to h_4. Thus, it can be seen that the effects of taxation are not as straightforward as might appear at the first sight.

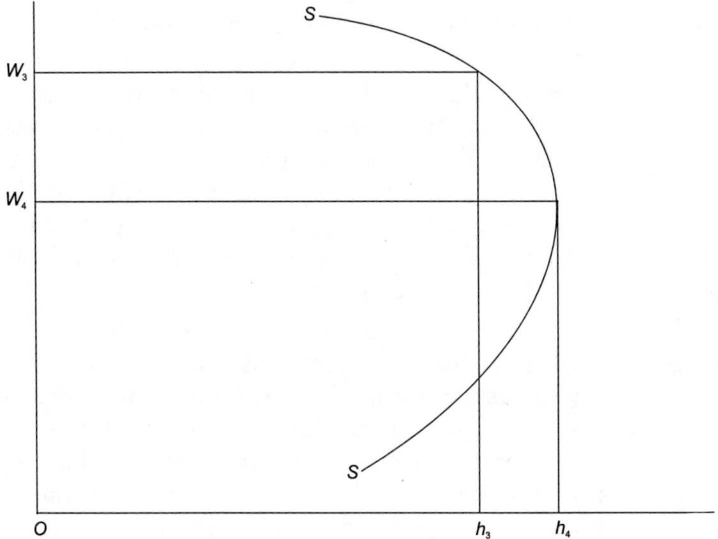

Fig. 7.6: Backward Bending Labour Supply Curve

The effect of a tax on wage income can be broken down into an income effect and a substitution effect. The income effect shows the reaction of taxpayer to vary his work effort as a result of the reduction of his income following the imposition of an income tax. It is normally supposed to be positive and enables a taxpayer to work hard to earn the same amount of income or more so as to remain on previously attained level of welfare. The extent of the income effect is determined by the proportion of an individual's gross income which goes in tax, that is, the *average* rate of tax. In case of substitution effect, a taxpayer is inclined to prefer leisure to work, since compared to the pre-tax position, in the post-tax position there will be an increase in the attractiveness of leisure relatively to work following the marginal benefit from work falling. Here no additional income is earned and, therefore, no tax is paid. A tax which reduces the marginal benefit from work will normally have a substitution effect which discourages work effort. In the case of an income tax, the extent of the substitution effect is determined by the *marginal* rate of tax. The theory, therefore, leaves us unable to predict the overall effect of tax change on the supply of labour as income and substitution effects usually work in opposite directions.

The substitution and income effects can be shown by using indifference curve technique. Here the assumptions made for the analysis of the supply curve of labour will be retained. In addition, it is assumed that both leisure and consumption are superior goods, their demand rising as income rises. In Fig. 7.7, taxpayer's choice between work and leisure is represented by *AB*. Before any tax is imposed he will choose to spend OL_1 hours of leisure, leaving time to earn OE_1.

If a proportional income tax is imposed on his income, the budget line will now swivel inwards to *CB* altering the trade-off between earnings and leisure. We shall look at the situation where the individual works harder as a result of the tax. Therefore, let us suppose that he moves to point P_3 and takes a reduced amount of leisure OL_3. The income effect can be removed by compensating the individual with an amount just sufficient to make him well-off as he would have been without the tax. In other words, his income needs to be increased so that he could just attain his former indifference curve I_1. This can be done by shifting the new budget line upwards until it is tangent to I_1. This is shown by *DF*. This line must be parallel to *CB* because we wish to retain the post-tax trade-off between earnings and leisure and to preserve the substitution effect.

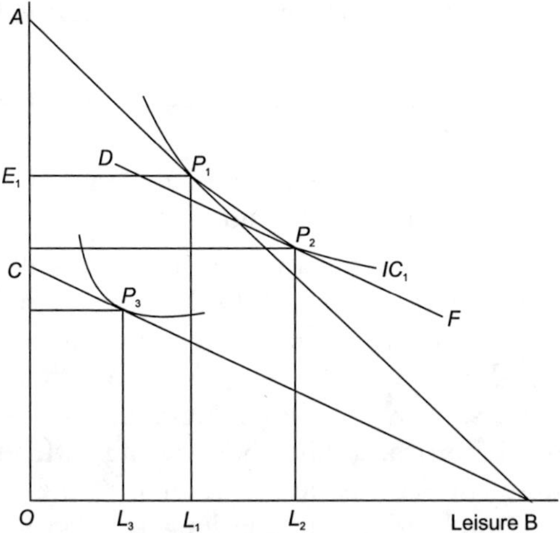

Fig. 7.7: Income and Substitution Effects

The substitution effect can now be seen as the movement from P_1 to P_2 around the indifference curve as the individual substitutes more leisure for less work. In Fig. 7.7, the individual would take an amount of OL_2 of leisure after the income tax was imposed rather than OL_1.

The income effect can be seen as operating in the opposite direction and encourages the individual to work hard. The individual taxpayer prefers taking OL_3 of leisure rather than OL_2. If the income effect predominates the taxpayer would prefer less leisure. On the contrary if the substitution effect prevails the taxpayer prefers more leisure and less work.

On account of imposition of a proportional tax, a certain amount of income, depending upon the rate of tax, is taken out from the pocket of a taxpayer and it is transferred to the public exchequer. Consequently, as we know it well, the taxpayer in post-tax scenario finds himself in a position where he spends and saves less than before. It does have some effect on the supply of labour. Every additional unit of labour supply brings in more money of which certain part is taken away by taxes. A taxpayer will examine the issue from four different angles:

1. Earn less by reducing labour supply and thereby pay less in tax.
2. Earn more by increasing labour supply and pay more tax.
3. Remain indifferent and maintain the same levels of income and labour supply.
4. Earn more but report less of the earned income and thereby resort to tax evasion.

On a cursory glance, the above mentioned issues appear to be simple, in reality these are not. Ordinarily, an individual has less control over his own supply of labour. Further, tax is not the only consideration in deciding the issue of increasing or reducing labour supply. One has to note interplay of a host of other factors. Empirical studies have found different answers to the above-mentioned issues. Particularly, the fourth issue has damaging implications. In the long run, on account of a consistent evasion, a huge parallel economy operates side by side with official economy wherein different fiscal tools, including taxation, lose their effectiveness.

Without going into the complexities associated with the response of an individual taxpayer, let us, on a very simple theoretical framework, try to examine the effect of a proportional income tax on the supply of labour under the assumption that a taxpayer has full control over his labour supply. He is free to choose, depending upon his personal requirements, a suitable combination of work effort and leisure. It is possible for him to substitute between work effort and leisure; more the leisure less is the work effort and *vice versa*.

In Fig. 7.8, work effort is measured on *OX* axis and leisure is measured on *OY* axis. The pre-tax budget line is *AB* on which the taxpayer is in equilibrium at point *E* where *OW* is amount of work and *OL* amount of leisure is enjoyed by the taxpayer. The imposition of a proportional income tax shifts the budget line to *EF* which would have been *CD* [parallel to *AB*] under a lump-sum tax. This disturbs his preferred combination of work effort and leisure. Other things remaining same, a taxpayer favours more units of leisure than before, i.e., OL_2 for the simple reason that any additional increase in income, following an increase in labour supply, adds to his tax liability. An interesting point to note here is that more units of work are substituted for less units of leisure.

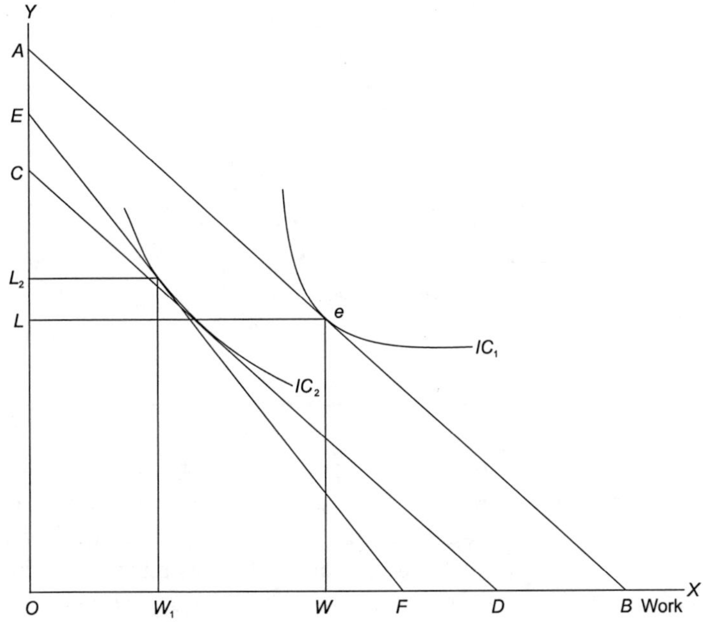

Fig. 7.8: Income Tax and Flexible Labour Supply

The other dimension is examined as under. In the Fig. 7.9 the units of work are measured on *OX* axis and units of income on *OY* axis. *OA* is the opportunity line before tax and *OD* is the opportunity line after the imposition of a simple proportional income tax. It cannot be said *a priori* whether the chosen point on *OD* will involve more or less work being done than before. It depends upon the interplay of various possibilities as mentioned above. The case illustrated in the Fig. 7.9 is that the taxpayer increases the amount of work by *XS*. He raises post-tax income slightly higher at *OT* than it would have been at *OU* if he had remained unmoved by the imposition of the tax. He is, of course, still much worse-off than he was in the pre-tax position when he did OX of work for OY of income.

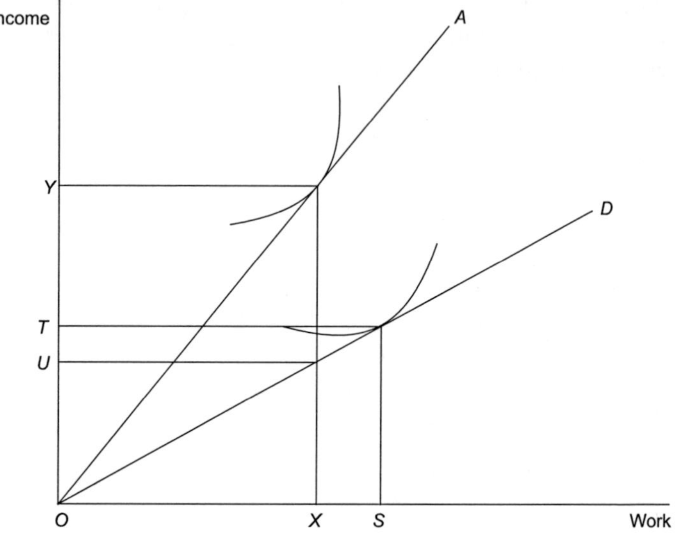

Fig. 7.9: Income Tax and Labour Supply

At this juncture, it is also important to note the composition of wage-package. Normally it has two components: (i) payment in-cash and (ii) perks and perquisites. If cash-benefits only are taxed and perks and perquisites are not taxed or lightly taxed, a taxpayer may prefer latter without reducing labour supply.

A Direct Personal Expenditure Tax

An expenditure tax is a tax upon the consumption component of income. By definition, an expenditure tax excludes all forms of savings and only consumption is considered for the purpose of taxation. It is also necessary here to distinguish sharply a direct personal expenditure tax from an indirect tax on expenditure, such as VAT, which is levied on commodities and not on the persons.

Let us discuss likely effects of an expenditure tax upon savings, spending, supply of work effort, etc., in comparison with an income tax yielding the same amount of tax revenue from the individual in question. For the sake of simplicity and comparison it is assumed that the direct expenditure tax is a simple proportional tax.

Effect of an Expenditure Tax on Savings

In the following Fig. 7.10, consumption is measured on *OX* axis and savings on *OY* axis.

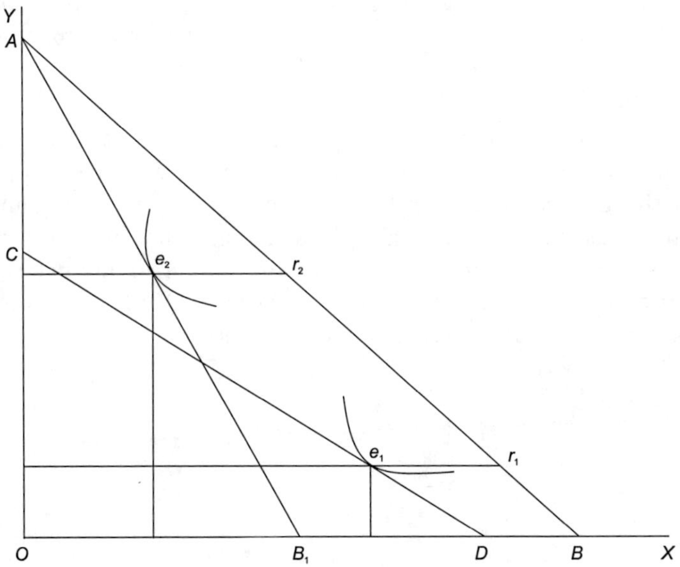

Fig. 7.10: Expenditure Tax and Savings

The introduction of a simple proportional income tax shifts the budget line from *AB* [pre-tax position] to *CD* [involving double taxation]. The new budget line *CD* is, therefore, not parallel to *AB*. On this budget line, the chosen point is e_1 and tax revenue is r_1e_1. As before, this tax favours consumption to savings. Let us now consider the case of an equal-yield expenditure tax. Since an expenditure tax excludes all forms of savings, the post-tax budget line starts from *A* and touches the horizontal axis *OX* at point B_1. The preferred position on AB_1 is e_2 where equal-revenue condition is satisfied. This amounts to say that the individual will save more and consume less than before. He is better-off than before as he finds himself on a higher *IC* at point e_2.

Effect of an Expenditure Tax on Work Effort

Let us now study the effect of a simple proportional expenditure tax on work effort, i.e., supply of labour. Here we come across an interesting situation. The earning of more income by increasing the supply of work effort does not in itself increase the liability of an individual to the expenditure tax. It is only when some or all of income is spent that an individual starts attracting tax liability.

In the following Fig. 7.11(A)[1], it is assumed that consumption is fixed at OO_1 level. As leisure is given up, i.e., as the individual moves from *B* towards *O*, more income is earned as indicated by *AB*. This income first goes to meet consumption expenditure in the segment of *AB* lying below the horizontal axis from O_1. Once it exceeds OO_1, it is saved. It may be also recalled here that under a lump-sum tax, the post-tax

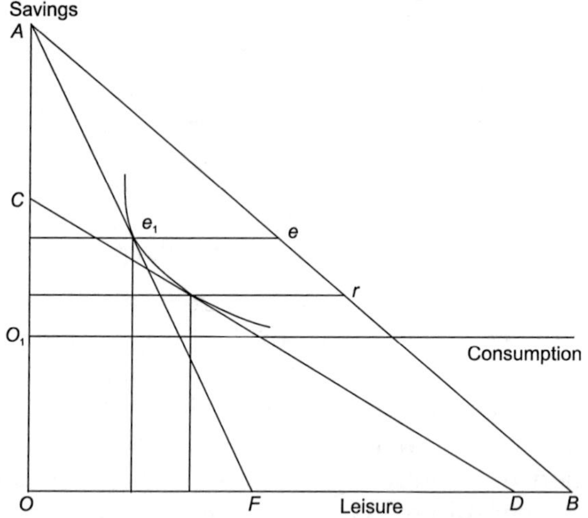

Fig. 7.11(A): Expenditure Tax and Work Effort

1. In the classroom while explaining this Figure, it is necessary to split it into two panels, one explaining imposition of income tax and the other explaining expenditure tax.

budget line happens to be parallel to the origin but not in case of other taxes. As explained earlier, a simple proportional income tax shifts *AB* to *CD* which is not parallel to *AB* because of its "swing" towards savings indicating double taxation of savings. The point of equilibrium is *e* and tax yield is *er*. Now we have to introduce a simple proportional expenditure tax of equal yield. In this case, the budget line starts from *A* indicating complete exclusion of savings from the tax net. This is necessary because by definition, an expenditure tax excludes all forms of savings. Such being the case, the new budget line originating from *A* takes a steep fall indicating heavy burden on consumption in order to satisfy equal revenue condition. On this new budget line *AF,* the equilibrium position is e_1 and tax revenue is e_1r_1 [= ee_1]. We reach the conclusion that in case of an equal-revenue expenditure tax a taxpayer saves more and works more. He is on a higher indifference curve.

In Fig. 7.11(B), savings are held constant at OO_1 level. Again, as leisure is given up some amount of income is earned which goes first to finance savings and then consumption. The imposition of a proportional income tax shifts *AB* to *CD* whereas when an equal-yield expenditure tax is imposed; the budget line originates from *F* and touches the vertical axis at point *G* indicating a heavy burden on consumption component

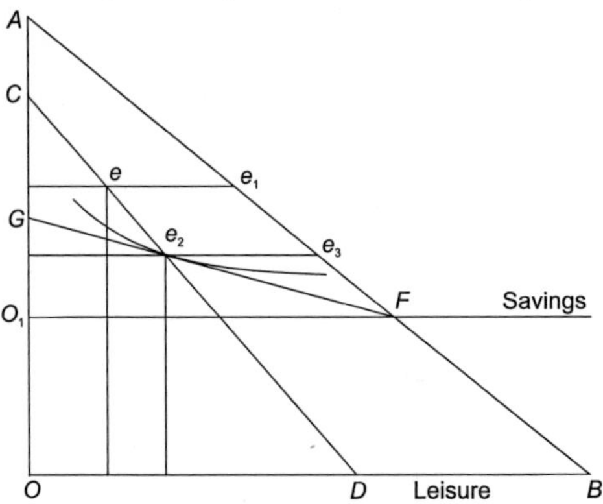

Fig. 7.11(B): Expenditure Tax and Work Effort

of income. On this budget line *FG* the equilibrium point is e_2 and tax revenue is e_2e_3 [= ee_1]. Here the taxpayer consumes less and works less. He is on a lower indifference curve.

Thus, we arrive at two different results depending upon the assumption we make:

1. Under a simple proportional expenditure tax, a taxpayer saves more and works more when consumption is held constant.
2. When savings are held constant, a taxpayer consumes less and works less.

The whole issue boils down to the tax treatment of savings. An important policy implication is that there should not be any control by the government either on the form or on the volume of savings. Of course, an income tax favours consumption and expenditure favours savings, the real issue to decide is that what should be favoured? Should we favour addition to the savings or depletion of savings? In the light of requirements of an economy, a suitable decision may be taken.

Incidence of Taxation

8

Objective: To study nature, scope, different notions and significance of incidence of taxation.

Organization: Meaning of Incidence; difference between incidence and effect; notions of incidence; tax incidence and elasticities of demand and supply; importance of study of incidence.

The Meaning of Incidence

There are two important issues which must be understood in any intelligent discussion on tax policy. First, whatever may be the type of tax; it is eventually paid from the streams of individual income. Second, the person upon whom the tax is originally imposed is not necessarily the person who bears its burden. Such being the situation, the tax theory must offer explanation of these two issues otherwise undesired results will be obtained.

When a tax is levied, its first impact will be felt by the subject of the tax, be it a person or a company or an institution that actually makes the tax payment. The person, or as the case may be, may absorb the tax himself or he may, if possible, shift the burden to someone else. In either case there will be a series of secondary effects of more or less economic significance.

Imposition of tax on the original subject will affect his disposable income and thereby his demand for different goods and services directly and productive factors indirectly. Shifting the burden to someone else implies a change in disposable income of others. If the tax results in a higher price, the buyers will bear it and will have less disposable income to spend for other products. If the shifting the tax results in lower physical volume of transactions of taxed commodity, the productive factors engaged in producing taxed-good will experience lower income. Thus, whether tax is shifted or not and wherever the incidence of tax is, a chain of economic effects sets in motion.[1] In this context, we need to understand three terms so commonly used. These are:

1. Impact
2. Shifting
3. Incidence

1. Impact: It refers to the point of original assessment of a person/company/institution. It is at this place, depending upon tax rate, that some impact of tax is felt. It is possible that an individual upon whom the tax is imposed in the first place may not be in a position to transfer the burden to others. Here, impact and incidence are on the same person. This happens mostly in case of direct taxes.

2. Shifting: In case where the first person is in a position to transfer the burden to someone else, then the shifting of tax is supposed to have taken place. This normally happens in case of manufacturers/sellers/service-providers who shift the burden of a tax to their consumers/customers even though they first experience its impact. The shifting of tax burden is normally of two types namely the forward shifting and the backward shifting.

(i) *Forward Shifting:* Forward shifting of a tax will involve a change in the price of taxed-commodity from what it otherwise would have been. Normally, prices rise when tax is shifted forward. It all depends upon the ability of original taxpayer to shift the burden forward to someone else. The most common example cited here is that of a wholesaler who shifts tax burden to the retailer who in turn passes it on to the final consumer.

---

1. Taylor, Philips, *op. cit.*, p. 306.

(ii) *Backward Shifting:* Backward shifting of a tax is not as common as forward shifting. It is, however, of immense theoretical significance for it helps us to learn about the negative impact of taxation on overall economy. The backward shifting occurs when the price of taxed commodity remains same but the burden is borne by the seller or by the factors of production. For example, a producer may force his workers to accept lower wages following the imposition of tax on the commodity produced by his firm. Such a happening will generate a series of side effects, typically adverse.

3. Incidence: In the light of observations made as above, it is maintained here that the tax incidence refers to the final or ultimate resting place of a tax. In the opinion of Seligman, tax incidence is "the settlement of tax burden on the ultimate taxpayer".[2] Another author, Otto von Mering, defines tax incidence as "the locale of final burden of tax. The further effects which may follow the placing of the ultimate burden of tax on certain persons or groups are not the part of theory of shifting".[3]

Difference between Incidence and Effect

There is a subtle difference between incidence and effect of a tax. Incidence refers to final or ultimate burden of a tax on a person/institution/company. The effect refers to an observable fact beyond final burden. For example, a tax reduces disposable income of a person on whom the incidence rests. He may be forced to reduce or postpone his present consumption. This may have ramifications for others productive agents in the economy. The demand for products and their factors get affected. It may also lead to loss of incentive, motivation, efficiency and flight of capital and other factors from heavily taxed sectors to relatively low taxed areas. It is, therefore, maintained here that the effect may be felt not only by those

2. Seligman, Edward, "Introduction to the Shifting and Incidence of Taxation" in *Readings in Economics of Taxation*, American Economic Association, George Allen and Unwin, London, 1959, pp. 171-201.
3. Otto von Mering, *The Shifting and Incidence of Taxation* quoted by K.P.M. Sundharam and K.K. Andley in *Public Finance: Theory and Practice*, S. Chand & Company, New Delhi, 2003, p. 202.

who pay taxes but also by those who do not pay taxes. The end-effect of incidence may be much greater than the revenue collected. In real terms, loss to taxpayers as well non-taxpayers may be much greater than the gain to the treasury.

In brief, it can be summed up here that the impact of tax is an initial phenomenon; shifting is an intermediate process and incidence is the final resting place of a tax. The effect is an occurrence beyond incidence. Any study of incidence ignoring the end-use of resources would be partial only as it does not encompass the total effect.

Dalton's Classification

In the area of incidence of taxation, the contribution of Hugh Dalton is worth studying. He is mainly responsible for bringing out the real nature of incidence of tax and for distinguishing it from the effects of a tax. He writes: "To every shilling of revenue raised, there corresponds a shilling of direct money burden or incidence falling upon someone."[4] The problem of incidence is to discover the person or persons who ultimately pay this one shilling. All other considerations relating to tax imposition may be regarded as effects. Dalton is of the view that the imposition of a tax leads to two types of burden on the people, *viz.*, money burden and real burden. This can be better understood with the help of Chart 8.1.

Money burden refers to the amount of tax paid by a taxpayer to the government. Money burden may be further divided into two types namely, direct money burden and indirect money burden. Direct money burden is the actual amount of tax in terms of money paid. Indirect money burden refers to a situation where a taxpayer may be required to part with a larger amount than the rate of tax warrants. For example, in addition to the tax actually paid, the taxpayer may be required to pay consulting fee to the tax consultant. In case of an individual, the amount may be meager but for companies it may turn out to be very huge.

---

4. Dalton Hugh, *Principles of Public Finance,* Routledge and Kegan Paul, London, 1936, p. 36.

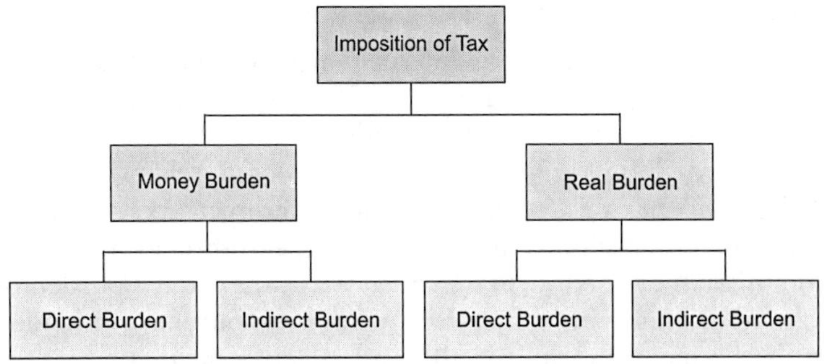

Chart 8.1: Types of Tax Burden

According to Dalton, the real burden of a tax relates to the sacrifice which the imposition of a tax entails on taxpayers. Real burden may be also divided into two types namely, direct real burden and indirect real burden. The direct real burden signifies the sacrifice of economic welfare whereas the indirect real burden refers to a reduction in consumption of a commodity following the imposition of a tax.

Mrs. Hicks' Classification

Mrs. Ursula Hicks in her book, *Public Finance*, has explained two types of incidence namely, the formal incidence and the effective incidence. In her opinion, formal incidence refers to the money burden of taxes. It rests with those taxpayers who initially pay taxes. Effective incidence refers to the broad effects of a tax. She writes: "In order to discover full economic consequences of a tax, we have to draw and compare two pictures, one of the economic setup (tax distribution of consumers' wants and income and allocation of factors) as it is with the tax in operation; the other of a similar economic setup but without the tax. It is convenient to call the difference between these two pictures, the effective incidence of the tax."[5] Explained in this way, it can be said that whereas the concept of formal incidence is narrow the notion of effective incidence is comprehensive.

5. Hicks, Mrs. Ursula, *Public Finance*, Pitman, New York, 1947, p. 158.

Taxation Enquiry Commission's Version

Mrs. Hicks's definition of incidence was adopted by the Taxation Enquiry Commission [1953-54]. This Commission was set up under the Chairmanship of John Matthai. It was the first to undertake a systematic and comprehensive study of the incidence of Central and States' indirect taxes on rural and urban households in different expenditure groups. The Commission defined formal incidence as "the money burden of taxes as resting with subjects on whom the burden is intended by the taxing authority to fall" and effective incidence as "the real or final distribution of tax after its shifting in consequence of changing demand and supply conditions of the taxed commodity or service".[6]

Modern Concept of Incidence

The above-mentioned concepts of incidence are normally referred to the traditional concepts. These have certain limitations. For example, following the imposition of a tax, only demand and supply do not change but disposable incomes also change and taxpayers get shifted from one spending group to the other. Tax may be a small factor exerting less powerful effect, there may be other factors much more significant than tax itself. Further, the traditional approach takes into account only the revenue side of the budget while ignoring the expenditure side. Thus, it is lopsided. A true incidence must deal with both sides of the budget.

Realizing above-mentioned limitations in the traditional approach, Mahler writes: "Initially, economists tended to limit the problem of incidence to one ascertaining the effect of the tax on the price of taxed article—all other reactions to the tax being classified as effects. Modern economists have tended to consider the problem of incidence as encompassing the distributional results of the tax. Thus, incidence is defined as the pattern of the final distribution of the burden of the tax among various income groups."[7] A similar view is expressed by George Break. He writes: "Modern incidence theory makes a

6. The Report of TEC, p. 45.
7. Mahler, Walter R., *Sales and Excise Taxation in India*, Orient Longman, New Delhi, 1970, p. 51.

basic distinction between the tax incidence on the sources of income side of household budgets and incidence on the uses-of-income side. Of fundamental importance is, how the burdens of different taxes are distributed vertically according to family income."[8]

Wicksell and other Swedish economists have given a new interpretation to the concept of incidence free from all ambiguities associated with traditional concept.[9] Following their foot-steps, Musgrave and Musgrave have provided a new version of incidence.

Musgrave's Classification of Incidence

Musgrave and Musgrave have propounded the following concepts of incidence[10]:

1. Statutory Incidence
2. Economic Incidence
3. Absolute Tax Incidence
4. Differential Tax Incidence
5. Budget Incidence

The above concepts are briefly explained as under:

1. Statutory Incidence: Musgrave and Musgrave maintain that taxes are not voluntary payments but mandatory impositions, payable in line with whatever tax statute has been legislated. Once legislated, they become mandatory levies, imposing burden which the taxpayer will try to avoid or pass on to others.

2. Economic Incidence: Following the process of shifting of tax burden there is a chain of adjustments. This may lead to a final distribution of the burden or economic incidence which differs greatly from the initial distribution liabilities or statutory incidence.

---

8. Break, George F., "Incidence and Economic Effects of Taxation" in Alan S. Blinder, et al. (ed.), *The Economics of Public Finance*, The Brooking Institution, Washington D.C., 1974, p. 120.
9. Gupta, J.R., *Public Economics in India: Theory and Practice*, Atlantic Publishers & Distributors, Pvt. Ltd., New Delhi, 2007, p. 178.
10. Musgrave and Musgrave, pp. 236-39.

3. Absolute Tax Incidence: Here the distributional effects of a particular tax are examined while holding public expenditures constant. Suppose that income tax rates are raised and more tax revenue is collected without there being a corresponding change in expenditure. Here one can hardly overlook the macro effects which follow from the resulting decline in aggregate demand. This decline may lead to unemployment, decline in price level or reduced rate of inflation. Each result will have its distributional implication which cannot be separated from those of the tax change itself. At closer consideration, the concept of absolute incidence is not a satisfactory one.

4. Differential Tax Incidence: Here one might examine the distributional changes which result if one tax is substituted for another while total revenue and expenditure are held constant. For example, the government may replace $1 billion of income tax revenue with a cigarette excise yielding an equivalent amount. Households whose income tax is reduced will gain, while others with high cigarette purchases will lose. Going beyond this, tobacco growers and cigarette workers will lose while others producing the output purchased by former income taxpayers stand to gain. The resulting total change in the state of distribution is referred to as "differential incidence". In the opinion of Musgrave and Musgrave, the concept of differential incidence also applies when we compare alternative ways of raising or lowering revenue. This view of tax incidence is particularly useful because actual tax policy decisions usually involve such issues.

5. Budget Incidence: Here changes in household positions are examined which result if the combined effects of tax and expenditure changes are considered. The income available to particular household for private use will now be affected not only by tax but also by expenditure measures of various layers of government. Thus, the expenditure side of the budget has its effects on private incomes as do taxes. Since tax and expenditure effects occur simultaneously, they cannot be separated to have a broad view.

Here we may add two more concepts namely dynamic incidence and static incidence. The concept of dynamic incidence is an improvement over the notion of static incidence. It is maintained here that immediate redistribution is the concern of static incidence where redistribution in the context of current incomes only is studied. Long-term redistribution is the subject of dynamic incidence. A tax redistributes incomes not only immediately after it is imposed but in all succeeding years as well. There is every possibility that a given tax system may be progressive in relation to redistribution of annual incomes but it may be regressive in relation to redistribution of lifetime incomes.

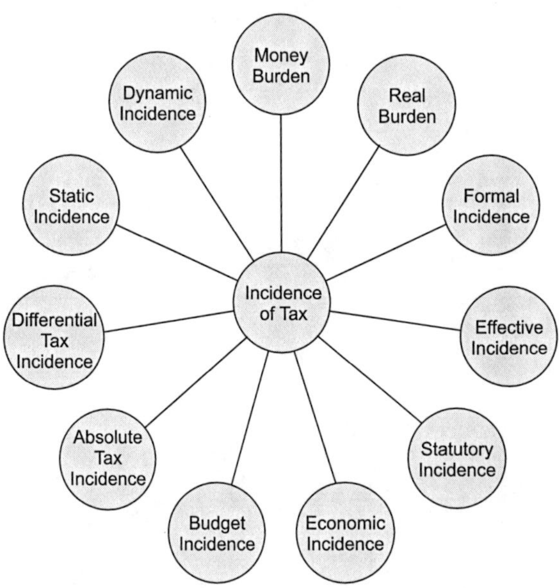

Chart 8.2: Different Concepts of Incidence

The Chart 8.2 enumerates different notions of tax incidence discussed so far.

Incidence and Partial Equilibrium Analysis

We should note that the incidence of a tax depends upon host of factors. The important, among others, are: rate structure, base, coverage, demand and supply elasticity, market condition, overall economy's response, etc. Some serious lessons for policy formulations can be learnt by studying tax incidence in the context of different elasticities of demand and supply. Some cases are examined as under:

1. Perfectly Elastic Demand: In Fig. 8.1, *DD* is perfectly elastic demand curve. Here the demand curve is parallel to *OX* axis. Following the imposition of a tax, supply curve SS shifts backward to S_1S_1. The distance between the two supply curves shows the amount of tax per unit. Whatever may the level of amount, the $O\ Q_1\ Q\ X$ tax per unit remains same and, therefore, S_1S_1 is parallel to *SS*. Price remains unchanged at *OP*; quantity demanded decreases from *OQ* to OQ_1 and entire burden is on the seller. He is confronted with the reduced demand for his product.

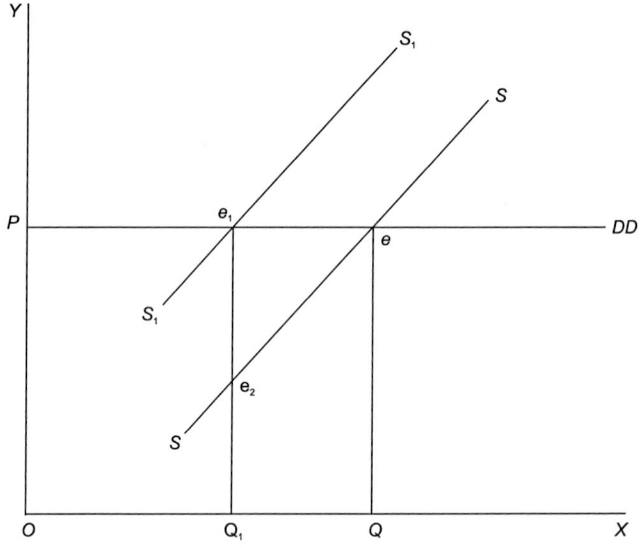

Fig. 8.1: Perfectly Elastic Demand

2. Perfectly Inelastic Demand: Let us now consider the case of a commodity whose demand is perfectly inelastic as depicted in Fig. 8.2. Here, the demand curve happens to be parallel to *OY* axis.

Following the imposition of tax, the price goes up from *OP* to OP_1. Since the demand is inelastic, the quantity demanded does not decline. It remains same at *OQ* level only. Consequently, the entire burden is passed on to the final consumer. He is made to purchase the same quantity, i.e., *OQ*, at a higher price than before.

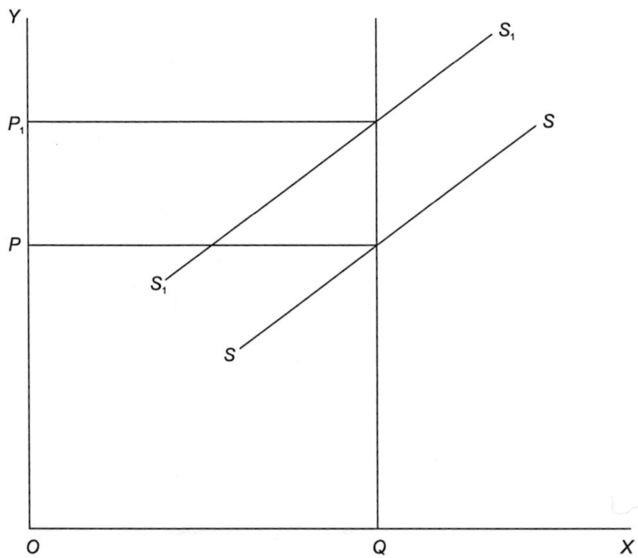

Fig. 8.2: Perfectly Inelastic Demand

3. Elastic and Inelastic Demand: Let us now try to understand tax incidence under different degrees of elasticity of demand. Here we consider the cases of elastic and inelastic demand in the Fig. 8.3.

Following the imposition of tax, there is an increase in price and the supply curve shifts backward from *SS* to S_1S_1. In case of elastic demand the extent of fall in demand is greater than the rise in price. And where the demand is inelastic, the buyer is made to purchase less than before at high price.

The whole discussion, as above, is summarized as under:

1. Where demand is perfectly elastic, the whole incidence is on sellers.
2. Where demand is perfectly inelastic, the whole incidence is on buyers.

3. Where demand is elastic, greater incidence is on sellers.
4. Where demand is inelastic, greater incidence is on buyers.

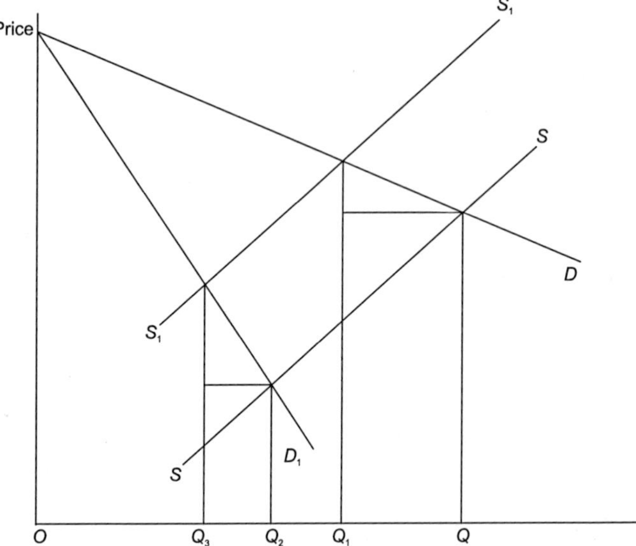

Fig. 8.3: Elastic and Inelastic Demand

In brief, it can be said that the extent of incidence greatly depends upon the type of elasticity of demand of a product confronting both the buyer and seller.

Incidence in General Equilibrium Analysis

Any study of tax incidence under partial equilibrium analysis does not help us to understand the issue as a whole. As the time is passing by, not only the national economy but the world economy too is becoming increasingly interdependent. Here, both the product and factor prices are affected by changes in the prices of other goods, substitutes in some cases and complementary in other cases. "Households not directly involved in the taxed market may lose or gain and those which are directly involved may become subject to further indirect effects."[11]

11. Musgrave and Musgrave, *op. cit.*, p. 257.

In the general equilibrium analysis, following the introduction of taxes, consumers buy less of taxed products, demand for their close substitutes may go up, other things remaining same. At the sources side, the derived demand for various factors of production changes creating repercussions in respective markets. Such repercussions continue until broadly diffused.

Aggregate demand and thereby, the levels of output, employment and prices are affected by the changes in the levels of taxation. Disposable incomes are affected. If tax reduction increases disposable income of a group of persons, it increases demand for goods and factor incomes of other groups through what is popularly known as multiplier effect. Reverse is true when tax rates are raised. Similarly, flow of investible funds and expected rate of return get affected. All these may have further distributional effects.

Considering the economy as a whole, we see that the overall effects of increase in government purchases and taxes by $X now involve the following[12]:

1. Disposable income of earners is reduced by $X.
2. Government revenue is increased by $X.
3. Benefits from public services are increased by $X.
4. Benefits from private services are reduced by $X.
5. Earnings from production for sale to private buyers are reduced by $X.
6. Earnings from production sold or services rendered to government are increased by $X.

Importance of Study of Tax Incidence

The importance of study of tax incidence is growing significantly for the reason that interest in the effect of budget on allocation, stabilization and income redistribution has stimulated many researchers to undertake tax and benefit incidence studies. Its importance was realized as early as 1899 when two out of fifteen questions relating to the reforms of local taxation in England were concerned with it. One of the

---

12. Musgrave and Musgrave, *op. cit.*, p. 239 with some alterations in ordering.

two questions was related to determining the real incidence of taxation as distinguished from primary or apparent incidence. The other dealt with the real incidence in the case of: (a) inherited house duty, (b) rates levied on houses and trade premises, (c) rats levied on agricultural land, (d) taxes on transfer of property, (e) taxes on trade and profits, and (f) death duties.[13]

Realizing the importance of study of incidence, Seligman writes that "the problem of incidence of taxation is one of the most neglected, as it is one of the most complicated subjects in economic science. Yet no topic in public finance is more important; for, in every system of taxation, the cardinal point is its influence on the community. Without correct analysis of the incidence of a tax, no proper opinion can be formed as its actual effect or justice."[14]

The study of incidence is important for several reasons. A few important reasons are as under:

1. The rule of the day is to tax persons according to ability to pay. In the interest of just distribution of the tax burden, it is essential to know on whom the ultimate burden of taxes in the end rests. The study of incidence helps us in this regard.

2. The study of incidence is significant in the sense that it helps us to know to what extent and under what circumstances the burden of tax is shifted on others. This helps taxation authority to locate the ultimate taxpayers. Once the expected incidence is known, a suitable rate structure may be developed to raise required amount of revenue.

3. The study of incidence helps governments to know the fact that the instrument of taxation has its own limitations in raising resources. It cannot be stretched too long for the reason that the burden of tax is also felt by those who do not, in the first place, pay a tax. It is maintained that persons who pay a tax are often less hurt by its imposition than those who pay no

13. Seligman, E.R.A., "Introduction to the Shifting and Incidence of Taxation", in *Readings in Economics of Taxation,* American Economic Association, George Allen and Unwin, London, 1959, pp. 171-201.

14. *Ibid.*

portion of it. The study of incidence is, therefore, important because it helps to understand wider effects of a tax.

There are, at the same time, certain noticeable limitations, for example:

1. A proper study of incidence is possible only when we know the demand and supply elasticities. Naturally, all the difficulties associated with the demand and supply elasticities silently creep into our analysis of incidence.

2. The study of incidence will be of limited significance in the context of certain fore-claimed objectives of economic policy. If the government is bent upon targeting certain groups/activities, the results of incidence analysis will be of limited use.

3. The conventional concept of incidence considers the direct money burden of taxes but it ignores the real effect through changes in income levels.

Nonetheless, the concept of incidence is important in its own place. Since it tries to understand the ultimate point of tax burden, the study of concept of incidence brings home the point that there are certain observable limits to the use of taxation as a means of revenue. It helps us to realize that efficiency cost may be high and the tax burden in real sense may far exceed the economic gain. In this context, the study of incidence helps tax authorities in designing appropriate rates.

Fringe Benefits Tax

9

Objective: To develop a case for the introduction of fringe benefits tax at company level.

Organization: Interest in fringe benefits; growth of fringe benefits; case for and against; revenue implications; valuation; choice of taxpaying unit; fringe benefits tax in India.

Interest in Fringe Benefits

In the area of taxation, the fringe benefits tax (FBT) is one of the latest innovations. Taxation of fringe benefits is desired to maintain equity, minimize inefficiency in resource allocation and raise more revenue. Currently, in several countries, these are taxed in the hands of employees. Here, an attempt is made to develop a case for a separate fringe benefits tax at the employer/company level on cash flow basis.[1]

Tax authorities around the globe have taken a serious note of the rapid growth of fringe benefits. The popular public sentiments are that the existing tax system is unfair, inefficient and unnecessarily complicated. Governments have been persuaded that tax reform is an urgent political need. It is hoped that in coming years, many countries would have low personal and corporate income tax rates. Since their budgets have no or a very little room for reducing expenditure, these countries need to broaden the tax base by eliminating or

1. Peerzade, Sayed Afzal, "Towards a Fringe Benefits Expenditure Tax", *Indian Journal of Economics,* Allahabad University, No. 283, 1991.

reducing a number of tax concessions, exemptions and other allowable deductions. A good number of tax theorists argue that unsystematic exemptions, concessions and deductions have led to a gradual shrinkage of the tax base. Their impact could be felt in terms of inequity, erosion of tax base and high marginal rates to obtain a desired amount of tax revenue.

Taxpayers and tax authorities as well are interested in the provision of fringe benefits. Taxpayers are interested because there is a good tradeoff between cash and non-cash components of the wage-mix which could be taken advantage of when tax rates are very high. Tax authorities are interested for the reason that an increased provision of fringe benefits leads to a gradual shrink in the tax base reducing chances of more revenue collections.

It is interesting to note that the inability to include fringe benefits in full in the personal income tax base was admitted at a time when the notion of income for tax purposes was in its formative stages. A number of Klienwatcher conundrums relating to the treatment of fringe benefits are famous. This issue came up for hearing before the House of Lords in the case Tennant vs. Smith (3 T.C. 158 H.L.), where the value of perquisites in kind which could not be converted into money was held non-taxable. In India, this decision was superseded by the Income Tax Act passed in 1922. Further, the Income Tax Act of 1961 has made perquisites in cash as well as in kind taxable subject to certain conditions and overall limits. The Act, however, has not defined perquisites but only a few items are included in that expression.

Fiscal theorists argue that an ideal personal income tax base should include in full the value of in-kind compensation. Schanz-Haig-Simons principle requires the inclusion of all sources of potential consumption. From S-H-S viewpoint, it makes no difference if the compensation received is in kind or in cash. If for one reason or the other, in-kind compensation is excluded, it then amounts to a departure from S-H-S principle. At present, in-kind compensation is not adequately covered by the tax laws. Companies providing fringe benefits to their employees claim tax deduction and at the recipient level too these are not fully taxed. Thus, their provision enjoys a double tax advantage, first at the company level and then at the recipient level.

Of late, much interest is evinced in the study of fringe benefits. This could be attributed to a desire on the part of tax authorities to broaden the tax base and to minimize inherent inequity in the system. Tax theorists argue that the issue of fringe benefits is assuming more importance because of the following reasons:

1. The proportion of total compensation that workers receive as wages and salaries has declined.
2. Revenue leakage on account of provision of fringe benefits is being noticed.
3. The provision of fringe benefits nullifies any attempt towards implementing a uniform pay structure.
4. As base shrinks the tax rate on non-excluded income has to increase in order to maintain a given level of revenue.

Causes of Growth of Fringe Benefits

The dramatic growth of fringe benefits since the Second World War may be attributed to a variety of reasons:

1. The unionization of labour force.
2. Preferential treatment of fringe benefits under personal income tax laws.
3. Savings that are made possible by the group purchases of some benefits.
4. Efforts on the part of employers to reduce labour flight.
5. Changing age composition of labour force. The effect of rising incomes pushing taxpayers into high tax brackets.

Fiscal theorists have disapproved the current tax treatment of fringe benefits on the ground of horizontal equity. They argue that two equals are treated unequally if one receives some untaxed income-in-kind while the other receives fully taxable compensation in-cash. Despite lack of guidance, the notion of horizontal equity is frequently invoked in public debate over tax policy.

When tax treatment is discriminatory, then employees at the top with an attractive fringe benefits package are more favourably treated than those who do not enjoy such a package. And, if at the same time, rate structure is progressive then exclusion of fringe benefits creates inequity. Tax reform programmes in several countries have admitted that much inequality has crept into the system because of a favourable tax treatment of fringe benefits. It was maintained that about 25 per cent of the remuneration package of a middle level manager was tax free in his hands as well as being deductible by the employer. In India, we see that there is uniformity in the basic salary structure of government departments, autonomous institutions and public sector units. However, it gets totally nullified by arbitrary and unequal distribution of fringe benefits. Consequently, inequity creeps into the system.

The Case for a Fringe Benefits Expenditure Tax

The case for a fringe benefits expenditure tax is developed in the following paragraphs:

1. It may be argued that the taxation of fringe benefits discourages companies to provide more non-cash benefits and they may be encouraged to switch over to the cash benefits. As and when more cash benefits are provided to the employees, their taxable incomes go up and many of them creep into high tax brackets. The gain is obvious. When companies start switching over to the cash-benefits or when more of the non-cash benefits are brought into the tax net then the tax base is clearly more comprehensive than before. It helps in reducing tax rates for a target amount of revenue. This will be in line with the world-wide trend in favour of low marginal rates. The comprehensive taxation of income may be expected to help keeping low the economic distortions.

2. The introduction of a fringe benefits expenditure tax helps us to remove anomalies that exist in the distribution of benefits at different levels. Consider for example, the case of house building loans. Employees of State Bank of India can borrow and amount equivalent to fifty times the basic salary. The rate of interest charged is also different from the one charged to others. Further, within the banking sector, the employees of other banks get a loan equivalent to seventy times the basic salary. The anomaly within the banking sector is quite clear. In sharp contrast to this, school teachers and college lecturers, for example, do not enjoy this facility. Further, similar discrepancies could be noted with regard to the other facilities such as consumption loans, leave travel concessions, festival advances and so on. When the provision of these benefits is tagged to a suitable tax, then employers and employees as well may make a suitable use of them as and when these are required and not simply because these benefits are available. In Hobessian sense, each employer/company could be taxed according to its willingness/capacity to provide a particular benefit from a pool of benefits. The principle of equity requires that either these anomalies should be removed or benefits should be made available to all employees. When neither is possible then, a serious attempt should be made to make these anomalies bear a cost at the employer/company level.
3. The introduction of a fringe benefits expenditure tax discourages inefficient allocation of resources. Of course it is a difficult task to monitor the actual use of concessional loans and other facilities yet, we may certainly claim that in case of loans for the purchase of luxury products there is some element of inefficient allocation. Very liberal loans from banks and financial institutions have led to a phenomenal increase in demand for housing pushing up reality prices. Similarly, liberal loans to purchase vehicles have led to

a phenomenal increase in their demand in addition to putting pressure on the supplies of diesel and petroleum products. Increased pollution, both of air and sound, is a good example of externality. Further, luxurious furnishings of residences and offices of chairmen, presidents and directors and other executives are usually done at the company's expenses. These are but a few indications of less efficient allocation of resources.

4. The fringe benefits expenditure tax may be an additional source of revenue to the government. Taking into consideration the enormous amounts involved and a large number of companies, institutions and organizations resorting to their provision, a tax even at nominal rate should yield a fair amount of revenue. This tax helps us to shift gradually the tax base from income to consumption.

The Case Against

There are at the same time, equally good arguments which do not support the introduction of a fringe benefits tax at the company level:

1. It may be that the taxation of fringe benefits achieves the goals of horizontal equity only when employees are taxed. While the existing laws cover their provision exhaustively, the real problem, however, is their full inclusion in the tax base.
2. At the company level, there are difficulties in separating out expenditure on fringe benefits from the total cost of production. Companies mix up the two in order to evade a tax there on. As compared to this, at the personal level, the identification of benefits received is easy so as to include them in taxable income.

The primary consideration of fiscal theorists and tax administrators has been to ensure a system where equity criterion is met. Within the income tax system, there are certain depressing areas which come in the way of realizing the goal of equity. One such is a lack of proper definition of income. Because of unclear definition of income and its defective measurement, an impression has gathered that the personal income tax as it is found today fall short of being an equitable tax. Similarly, tax laws do not define fringe benefits but only offer a list of what constitute these benefits. When it is noticed that their exclusion or partial inclusion adds to the inequity, then their inclusion in full and their comprehensive taxation could at least restore some equity.

Choice of Taxpaying Unit

Since the principle of equity requires that the fringe benefits should be taxed, an important issue, then, is the choice of taxpaying unit. Conventionally, fringe benefits are taxed at the personal level. It is the individual employee who is benefited most from the provision of fringe benefits. Strictly from accretion point of view, fringe benefits add to the spending power of recipient.

The main difficulty in taxing fringe benefits at the personal level is that their provision requires yearly valuation which by no means is any easy task. A few might complain that fringes were thrust upon them as a part of marketing strategy of the company without much regard to their personal tastes and preferences. Further, the provision of fringe benefits may also add to compliance cost. Recipients are required to keep a detailed account of benefits enjoyed. They need to have a perfect knowledge of retail and discount prices of benefits so as to compute gain in money terms and add it back to their incomes.

It is argued here that the compliance, valuation and administrative aspects heavily tilt the balance in favour of company as a taxpaying unit. When the flow of benefits gets taxed at the company level, it amounts to their indirect taxation at the level of employees. As a taxpaying unit, a company may be preferred to an individual for the following reasons:

1. In providing fringe benefits companies stand to gain because they “tie-up” employees by offering attractive

benefits and minimize the chances of their deserting the companies. Companies might use fringe benefits as a weapon of "selective discrimination" when law of the land does not permit "open discrimination".

2. Requiring companies to pay the fringe benefits tax is an administratively a feasible proposal. It is easier to calculate the value of different benefits provided. For example, if a fleet of motor cars is always available to a group of employees for their personal use, then it is not necessary to calculate benefits to each employee; instead cost to the company on account of private use of company cars is considered. Similarly, the total value of subsidized loans sanctioned to employees is treated as companies' expenditure on fringe benefits provision.
3. The tax liability is checked by a reference to only one tax return filed by the company in place of hundreds of returns required to be filed by employees. This not only reduces compliance costs, it also makes overall administration of fringe benefits tax simpler.
4. Taxing companies rather than employees has both political and policy advantages. There are at any point of time many more employees than companies. By bringing companies into the tax net, the government might hope to provoke less of an adverse voters' reaction. From policy viewpoint, the advantage is that the companies might be encouraged to shift from non-monetary to the monetary pay-package. Shifting the whole of compliance burden and valuation of fringe benefits to companies might help achieve this policy goal.
5. Since the fringe benefits tax is likely to be a relatively complex instrument, companies are more suited to cope with the record keeping and filing of return as would be necessary. Companies also have access to the services of accountants, tax experts, legal advisors

and others to ascertain properly provision of fringe benefits.

6. It would not be difficult for companies to append a separate report on fringe benefits for the reason that currently they are required to file a report which contains information regarding the gross salaries paid to their employees.

Thus, it is argued here that the compliance, valuation and other administrative aspects as discussed above make us to prefer employers/companies as taxpaying units. They, and not the individuals are better equipped with their professional and administrative manpower to comply with different provisions of fringe benefits tax.

This argument also does not hold ground that the separation of expenditure on fringe benefits from total manufacturing expenditure is difficult. The existing tax laws have already identified different benefits; the issue then is to ask companies to provide full information of their expenditure on the provision of fringe benefits. This should also be noted that when the market value of benefits is taken into account, it is, then, not difficult to collect a fringe benefits tax from employees/companies. This argument in fact goes in favour of considering companies/employers as the taxpaying units. Companies, because of their command over vast financial and administrative resources, are in a better position to pay this tax. After all they have an option. They may reduce expenditure on fringe benefits or change payment package in favour of cash benefits.

Valuation of Fringe Benefits

There are three different methods of valuation of fringe benefits:

1. Fair Market Price Method.
2. Employees Willingness Method.
3. Cost of Provision Method.

The fair market price method takes into consideration the retail value of fringe benefits. It is then added to the employees' income and taxed accordingly. This method appears to be very simple, nevertheless there are a few problems. Not all fringes are traded nor there is always a ready market to ascertain their proper value in money terms. As prices of different goods and services frequently fluctuate, we have to prepare an index number. Here, unwillingly, those difficulties creep into the picture which are commonly associated with the construction of index numbers. Another difficulty is that employers might understate prices of benefits procured from the market in order to evade the tax as and when a certain portion of fringe benefits is tax exempt.

The other method is to take note of employees' willingness to pay for benefits received. Here we estimate the amount which employees are willing to pay for the same goods and services in an open market. The amount so ascertained is added back to the taxable income of employees. When compared to the first method, the second method is found to be subjective. Here we have to know in detail employees tastes, preferences, likes and dislikes. Further, the willingness to pay for the same bundle of benefits may be different for different employees. Similarly, in case of a given employee, it is very likely to change as he moves up from a low to high-income bracket and from one age group to another.

The third method is to work out the cost of provision of fringe benefits to employers. A fringe benefits expenditure tax with suitable rates could be then imposed on full or a part of such expenditure. In a number of countries, employers/companies are required to file their annual reports at the end of each financial year. These reports while highlighting the performance of companies, provide information regarding gross salaries. A large number of companies pay perks and perquisites to all levels of employees. However, their proportion to cash-payment may be different at different levels. In case of chairmen, directors and other executives, the fringe benefits package is clearly spelt out. Companies and organization fear that there are all possibilities of losing efficient and experienced professionals if the pay package is not attractive and if it is not revised annually. The annual reports therefore are of a great use. This method could be preferred because of its objectivity and clarity. Companies may be asked to submit additional information of their expenditure on the provision of fringe benefits. This method is used in Australia and New Zealand, where a fringe benefits tax is imposed at the company level.

Introducing a Fringe Benefits Expenditure Tax in India

Income tax was introduced in India in the year 1860 and at that time income was taxable under four different heads namely, income from land property, including income from agricultural land and house property, income from professions and trades, income from securities and income from salaries and pensions. The Act of 1886 excluded agricultural income from the purview of income tax and in its place, income derived from sources other than agricultural was included. This schedule was very comprehensive and it covered among other industrial and commercial income and income from property.

The Income Tax Act of 1918 excluded non-monetary benefits from the purview of taxation. It followed the Tennant vs. Smith case as decided by the House of Lords in 1882. The exclusion was due to a ruling of Madras High Court that income should mean the income actually or constructively received. This ruling created difficulties both to the government and business community.

With the enactment of Income Tax Act of 1922, different components of fringe benefits were gradually brought into the tax net. A beginning was made with the inclusion of rent of the accommodation provided to the employees. Further, the rent free accommodation was considered as a taxable perquisite. A major change in the tax treatment of perquisites took place in the year 1955 when the Taxation Enquiry Commission recommended inclusion of fringe benefits in the interest of equity. Consequently, necessary amendments were made in the provisions concerning taxation of salaries.

The Income Tax Act of 1962 which came into effect from 1st of April 1962, replaced the Income Tax Act of 1922. It incorporated a more comprehensive definition of income than the earlier one in the Act of 1922. Here a provision is made to the effect that the value of any benefits, whether convertible into money or not received by a person in exercise of his business or profession shall be assessable in the hands of recipients as income. Rule 3 explains the method of computation of certain specific benefits such as furnished or unfurnished residence, motor cars or any other conveyance for the personal use, gas, water, electricity charges paid for the personal use. There is no tax on employers on account of the benefits provided. However, certain expenses are discouraged by restricting the permissible deductions such as entertainment and traveling allowances. Further, any sum paid by the employer in respect of any obligations which but for such benefits a payment would have been made by the employee whether directly or indirectly to a recognized provident fund or a deposit linked insurance plan to effect an assurance on the life of an assessee or to effect a contract for an annuity. When we propose company as a taxpaying unit, the desired coverage of fringe benefits should be as broad as possible. It should include such of the benefits which are at present excluded from the expression of perquisites under section 17(2). It should also include fringe benefits provision expenditure on such of the employees too who are not paying any income tax. This is for the reason that the taxpaying unit is a company and not an employee. In one form or the other, companies provide fringe benefits to all employees. It is, therefore, necessary to do away with the compartmentalization of employees into taxed and non-taxed categories.

It could be alleged here that in case of non-taxpaying employees, the fringe benefits provided to them should not be taxed because their salaries as such are not taxed. *Prima facie,* this is a forceful argument. Nevertheless, from equity view point, such a compartmentalization of employees should disappear. Further, we are not asking employees to pay tax on fringe benefits received, instead their company is asked to pay tax on its expenditure on benefits provided. The fact is that at the company level, fringe benefits are provided to all employees. An executive enjoys use of company car and an ordinary employee is picked up in the company van or bus. Similarly, luxuriously furnished accommodation is provided to the chairmen, directors and other executives whereas an ordinary employee is provided with a minimum accommodation facility.

In India, the Union Finance Minister in his budget 2005-06 speech announced the introduction of fringe benefits tax (FBT). It was regarded as the most significant proposal in the Finance Bill of 2005. It came into force from April 1, 2005. It was proposed to be collected at the rate of 30 per cent. India is not the only country to introduce this tax. Since long, it is in force in Australia and New Zealand.

In his budget speech, the Finance Minister noted that many perquisites given to employees were escaping from tax net. These benefits, he said, were of considerable material value and neither the employer nor the employee paid any tax on them. He, therefore, declared: "Where the benefits are fully attributable to the employee; that provision will continue. In addition, I now propose that where the benefits are usually enjoyed collectively by the employees, and cannot be attributed to individual employees, they shall be taxed in the hands of the employer". For this purpose, a new chapter XII-H is proposed to be inserted in the Income Tax Act containing sections of 115W to 115WL.

This has sparked off a huge debate amongst corporate and tax circles. Trade and industry have been unanimous in their opposition of FBT. Doubts have been raised that industry will be badly hit by the fringe benefits tax. It is estimated that an expenditure of Rs. 25,000 crores made by companies, etc., will come under the purview of fringe benefits tax.

Fringe benefits as outlined in Section 115WB of the Finance Bill mean any privilege, service facility or amenity directly or indirectly provided by an employer to his employees (including former employees) by reason of their employment. According to the Finance Bill, fringe benefits shall be deemed to have been provided if the employer has incurred any expense or made any payment for the purposes of:

entertainment; festival celebrations; gifts; use of club facilities; provision of hospitality of every kind to any person; maintenance of guest houses; conferences; employee welfare; use of health club, sports and similar facilities; sales promotion, including publicity; conveyance, tour and travel, including foreign travel expenses; hotel boarding and lodging; repairs, running and maintenance of motors cars; repairs, running and maintenance of aircraft; consumption of fuel other than industrial fuel; use of telephone; scholarships to the children of employees.

Under the proposed provisions, fringe benefit tax is payable by an employer who is either an individual or a Hindu Undivided family engaged in a business or profession; a company; a firm; an association of persons (AOP) or a body of individuals (BOI); a local authority; a sole trader or an artificial juridical person. The fringe benefits tax is payable by the employer even where he is not liable to pay income tax on his total income computed in accordance with the other provisions of this Act.

Following the introduction of fringe benefits tax (FBT), employers have started reviewing their salary structure. It may induce companies to withdraw some perquisites. This in turn may result in a further simplification of compensation structures, more in cash and less in kind. Compensation package will now have a new look; it will have limited heads, at the most five or six. Some companies may continue to offer these perks to senior level employees and bear the burden of the FBT; at other levels, they may resort to a consolidation of heads of pay and merging many odd reimbursements into basic pay. Some companies have been quick to respond to the treatment of expenses as fringe benefits. Perks have been merged with pay increasing the tax liabilities of employees. However, since there is demand for skilled manpower, an enlightened employer/company will not pull out all benefits at one go.

Value Added Tax

10

Objective: To understand meaning and functioning of a value added tax.

Organization: Understanding the term; introduction of VAT in different countries; working of VAT; major differences; variants of VAT; computation; popularity of VAT; advantages; economic effects of VAT; arguments against.

Understanding the Term

In recent years, the Value Added Tax (VAT) has emerged as one of the important fiscal innovations.[1] It has attracted huge attention of policy-makers, planners, tax theorists notwithstanding the attention it received from the business community at large. Around the world, nearly 130 countries are administering one or the other type of VAT.

Till recently, in a number of countries, the system of indirect taxation was considered to be complex on account of (1) multiplicity of taxes and (2) non-uniform rates particularly where several layers of government exist. These two have contributed to heavy compliance costs and cascading effect. The cascading effect is said to occur when there is tax on tax. In this context, Kelkar Committee has noted that these difficulties have led to substantial distortions, and the choice of

---

1. The present author has borrowed heavily from Mahesh Purohit's *Value Added Tax*, Fourth Edition, Gayatri Publications, New Delhi, 2006. Alan A. Tait's work *Value Added Tax*, McGraw-Hill Book Company, 1972, is also consulted.

production technologies and inputs in the country has become distorted.[2]

To understand the meaning of value added, it is necessary first to explain the term value added as used in economics.[3] In ancient times, when the economy was mainly barter, goods were produced locally and in most cases, for local consumption. Normally, the producer himself was the seller of his products. In contrast, modern system of production is highly complex involving acute division of labour, large scale production and a wide market for the output. The final product as handed down to the consumer does not represent the efforts of one production unit but a host of independent manufacturers, big and small. The value of final product as it reaches the customer represents the reward of the services of various factors of production rendered at different stages in the chain of production and distribution. The final value is the sum total of values added at different stages.[4]

It was a German scholar, by name F. Von Siemens, who advocated VAT as a substitute to the turnover tax (TOT) in the year 1918. Since then, academic interest in this tax has continued to develop. Enriching contributions were also made by Maurice Laure. The VAT is defined as: "A broad based tax levied on commodity sales up to and including at least the manufacturing stage, with systematic offsetting of tax on commodities purchased as inputs against that due on outputs."[5]

Over the years, several economists and tax reform committees have recommended introduction of VAT for several reasons, the most important being its neutrality. A tax is said to be neutral when it does not distort the choice

2. Government of India, Ministry of Finance, *Report of the Task Force on Implementation of the Fiscal Responsibility and Budget Management Act-2003,* 2004. It is also known as Kelkar Committee Report.
3. Ahuja Astha, *Value Added Tax: Indian and Global Experiences*, New Century Publications, New Delhi, 2004, p. 4.
4. *Ibid.*
5. Krishnan, V.S., *Indirect Tax Reforms: Challenge and Response,* Abhinav Publications, New Delhi, 2006, p. 57.

between income and consumption; between the purchase and consumption of two commodities; between leisure and work-effort and amongst different types of savings and investments. Since VAT is introduced at uniform rates throughout the country, it encourages internal and interstate trade without much irritation. Consequently, there would be optimum allocation of resources. Since it sans cascading effect, production efficiency would improve.

Introduction of VAT in Different Countries

Even though it was proposed in the year 1918, it took another thirty years for its introduction in France in 1948. From France, it went to its colonies in Western Africa (the Francophone countries) and from there to South America. The initial impetus for VAT came from the desire to have greater economic integration of the European Union. However, the real surge in the introduction of VAT took place in the 1980s and 1990s.[6] The following Table 10.1 traces year-wise introduction of VAT in a few selected countries.

Table 10.1: Introduction of VAT

Sl. No.	Country	Year of Introduction
1.	France	January 1948
2.	Denmark	July 1967
3.	Germany	January 1968
4.	Belgium	January 1971
5.	United Kingdom	April 1973
6.	Pakistan	November 1990
7.	Canada	January 1991
8.	Bangladesh	July 1991
9.	Egypt	July 1991
10.	South Africa	September 1991
11.	Russia	January 1992
12.	China	January 1994
13.	Nigeria	January 1994
14.	Australia	July 2000
15.	India (Federal) (States)	April 2001 April 2005

Source: Mahesh Purohit (2006).

6. Krishnan, V.S., *Indirect Tax Reforms: Challenge and Response,* Abhinav Publications, New Delhi, 2006, pp. 58-59.

From Table 10.1, it is clear that VAT is introduced in every major country of the world. As the time is flowing, more and more countries are introducing VAT to realize its intrinsic advantages. Indian government introduced it recently because of its own federal compulsions. Its performance, however, is quite satisfactory. It is collected at two rates, at four per cent and at twelve per cent, depending upon the type of commodity purchased.

Working of VAT

VAT is a tax levied on the value added of a commodity or service as it passes through different stages of production and distribution until it reaches the final destination of consumption. Here, tax is payable at each stage in a chain of stages right from collection of raw materials to the consumption of final product. At each stage, a certain value is added to the product/service and this "value added" is taxed and hence it is called VAT. It is also called a multi-point tax as against the single-point conventional sales tax. The revenue outcome, however, is not different. The total tax collected by the government under VAT will be exactly equal to the tax collected on the retail-selling price of the product/service by the retailer.

The notion of VAT revolves around the tax credit or tax rebate. The system provides for setting off the tax paid earlier. The VAT liability of a party is calculated by deducting input tax credit from tax collected on sales during the payment period. At each stage, VAT will be collected on the sale price at the rate applicable to the commodity. From the tax so collected, the seller will retain the amount of tax paid on purchases and remit the balance alone to the government. This process continues till the commodity or service reaches the final consumer. In this system, the tax remitted to the government at each stage will be tax on the value addition of the product or the service made by the seller. Thus, in a way, the VAT is a multiple point turn-over-tax (TOT) imposed at each stage of production and distribution of goods and services by business firms minus the tax paid on the purchase of goods and services from other firms. It, therefore, does not have cascading effect due to the system of deduction or credit mechanism.

VAT is a tax on consumption. The final total burden of the tax is fully and exclusively borne by the domestic consumer of goods and services. Since it is a tax on domestic consumption, no VAT is charged on goods exported. It is an alternative mechanism of collection of commodities-based indirect taxes. The essence of VAT is summarized as under[7]:

1. VAT is a multipoint sales tax with set-off for tax paid on purchase.
2. It is collected in installment at each stage of transaction from production to distribution.
3. It does not have cascading effect due to the system of deduction or credit mechanism.
4. It is tax on consumption. The final and total burden of the tax is fully and exclusively borne by the domestic consumer of goods and services.
5. No VAT is charged on goods exported.
6. It is in many respects equivalent to a last point retail sales tax.

It is interesting academically to note the working of VAT which is collected at different stages. To illustrate this, let us assume dealer A to be a raw material producer, B to be a manufacturer, C to be a wholesaler and D to be a retailer.[8] Dealer A sells his produce at Rs. 100 and pays tax at the rate of 10 per cent. The sale price of Rs. 100 is the purchase price for dealer B who is a manufacturer. This dealer will incur wages, salaries, other manufacturing expenses and to all this he adds interest and his own profit. Assume that after adding all these costs, his sale price is Rs. 200. On this sales price the tax at the rate of 10 per cent would be Rs. 20. Since dealer A has already paid tax on Rs. 100, dealer B gets credit for this tax. Therefore, his net VAT liability is Rs. 20 minus Rs. 10. That is, dealer B pays to the government Rs. 10 only. Similarly, the sale price of Rs. 300 by dealer C would have net liability of Rs. 10

7. Purohit, Mahesh, *op. cit.*, p. 6.
8. This example is adopted from Purohit, *op. cit.*, p. 4.

(Rs. 30 – Rs. 20 = Rs. 10) and the sale price of Rs. 400 by dealer D would also have net VAT liability of Rs. 10 (Rs. 40 – Rs. 30 = Rs. 10). This indicates:

1. VAT is collected at each stage of production and distribution.
2. On account of credit/rebate of the tax paid earlier, there is no cascading effect.
3. The burden of tax falls on final consumer only.

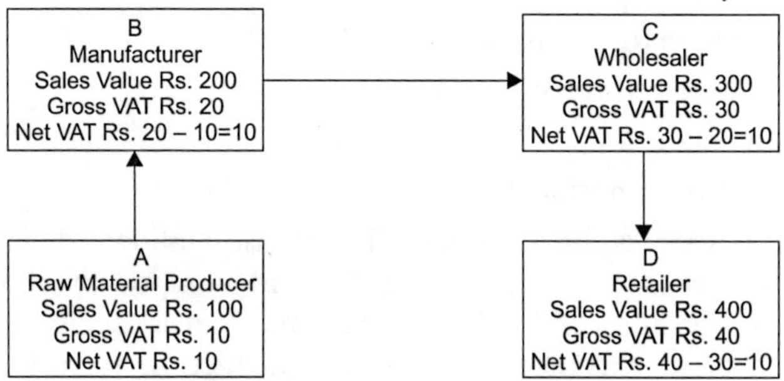

Chart 10.1: Different Stages of VAT

Major Difference Between VAT and Sales Tax

The Table 10.2 points out certain major differences between VAT and sales tax:

Table 10.2: Major Differences between VAT and Sales Tax

Sl. No.	Basis	Sales Tax	VAT
1.	Origin of Tax	Sellers pay tax	Consumers pay tax
2.	Assessment	Book based and checked by the officials	Self-assessment, dealers' assessment audited
3.	Accounting	No input tax credit is allowed	Input tax paid earlier by the registered dealer is set off against output tax and carry forward is also allowed
4.	Collection point	Single point	Multi point
5.	Book of Accounts	Sales registers and sales invoice are to be maintained	Sales registers and purchase registers to be maintained
6.	Closing stock valuation	Closing stock does not reflect true value as the tax component has already been added to it	Closing stock valuation is based on true value, i.e., actual and without tax components

(Contd.)

7.	Nature of tax	Sales tax is considered as hidden cost and the customer does not know how much tax is paid	Entire tax burden is reflected and tax paid by the customer is considered as transparent cost
8.	Visibility of tax	Concealed	Open
9.	Simplicity	Confusing because of numerous rates	Simple because of one or two rates

Source: Adopted from Raul, R.K. [2006].

Variants of VAT

There are three variants of VAT namely[9]:

1. Gross Product Variant
2. Income Type Variant
3. Consumption Type Variant

1. Gross Product Variant: This option allows deduction for all purchases of raw materials and components but no deduction is allowed for business inputs, that is, capital goods such as plant and machinery are not deductible from the tax base in the year of purchase. Depreciation on the plant and machinery is not deductible in the subsequent years. Thus, the economic base of gross product variant is equivalent to gross national product. In this variant of VAT, capital goods carry a heavier tax burden as they are taxed twice. Modernization and upgrading of plant and machinery are delayed due to this dual tax treatment.

2. Income Product Variant: In this option, deductions are allowed for purchases of raw materials and components as well as depreciation on capital goods. It provides an incentive to classify purchases as current expenditure to claim set-off. Net investment is taxed and, therefore, the economic base of the income variant is equivalent to net national product. In practice, however, problems arise regarding methods of measuring depreciation, which depends upon the life of an asset as well as on the rate of inflation.

3. Consumption Variant: This variant allows deduction for all business purchases including capital assets, that is, gross investment is deducted in the calculation of "value added".

9. Purohit, Mahesh, *op. cit.*, pp. 6-8.

The economic base of the tax, therefore, is equivalent to total private consumption. It neither distinguishes between capital and current expenditures nor specifies the life of the asset or depreciation allowance for different assets. This form is neutral between different methods of production, i.e., there is no tax liability due to the method of production. The tax is also neutral between the decision to save or consume.

Among the three variants of VAT, the consumption variant is most widely used. Most countries have adopted this variant. The reasons are obvious[10]:

1. It does not affect decision regarding investment because the tax on capital goods is also set-off against VAT liability.
2. This tax is neutral in respect of techniques of production (labour or capital-intensive).
3. It is more in harmony with the destination principle.
4. In the area of foreign trade, while imports are taxed all exports are exempt from taxation.
5. It simplifies tax administration by obviating the need to distinguish between purchases of intermediate and capital goods on the one hand and that of consumption goods on the other.
6. Since one or two rates of VAT are normally administered, the system as such would be simple to administer.

Methods of Computation of VAT

There are three methods of computing tax liability under VAT. These are as under:

1. Addition Method
2. Subtraction Method
3. Tax Credit Method

Under the addition method, value added is computed by summation of all the elements of value addition such as wages, profits, rent and interest, etc. This method is also known as

---

10. Purohit, Mahesh, *op. cit.*, p. 8.

income method. This is in line with the income method of calculating national income. The subtraction method estimates value added by means of the difference between the value of outputs and inputs. This is also known as product approach. The tax credit method is also known as invoice method under which deduction of tax on inputs is allowed from sales for each tax period. In practice, many countries are using this method for purpose of computing VAT liability.

Reasons for Growing Popularity of VAT

The popularity of VAT has increased over a period of time. The following Table 10.3 explains region-wise introduction of VAT.

Table 10.3: Region-wise Introduction of VAT

Year	Sub-Saharan Africa	Asia and Pacific	European Union	Central Europe and BRO	N. Africa and Middle East	American Continent	Small Islands
1969	1	0	5	0	0	2	0
1979	1	1	12	0	1	12	0
1989	4	6	15	1	4	16	1
2001 April	27 (43)	18 (24)	17 (17)	25 (26)	6 (21)	22 (26)	8 (27)

Source: IMF Staff Compilation.

Note: Figure in brackets is the total number of countries in each region.

Currently, the VAT is being administered in more than 130 countries of the world. A large number of other countries too are planning to switch over to VAT in the near future. This speaks about its immense popularity. VAT owes its popularity to the following reasons.[11]

1. Simple Tax Structure: VAT helps in simplifying the indirect tax system. In many countries, the pre-VAT commodity tax systems were very complicated. For example, Korea had 11 different kinds of indirect taxes before the adoption of VAT. There existed 53 different rate brackets amongst eight of these eleven indirect taxes.

2. Reduction in the Evasion of Tax: VAT requires that all the dealers must issue invoices. The subsequent

11. Purohit, Mahesh, *op. cit.*, p. 11.

dealer maintains these invoices in order to benefit from tax deduction. This enables the tax authority to cross check the declared transaction between taxpayers, consequently reducing the propensity to evade tax. In fact, the requirement of maintaining the vouchers works as a self-policing mechanism to prevent the evasion of tax.

3. Tax Neutrality: The most significant advantage of VAT is that it is neutral between commodities. This is for the simple reason that all through the country, for a specific group of commodities, only one rate is administered. Since only one rate operates, it does not affect choice between types of commodities and, therefore, it is held as neutral.

4. Efficient Allocation of Resources: As pointed out above, VAT is neutral for a specific group of commodity and, therefore, does not affect choice and the funds flow efficiently. Only such goods and services will be produced and marketed which are consistently demanded. This strengthens competition in that particular area of economic activity. Ultimately, consumer welfare level goes up for the reasons that they get best in quality at competitive prices.

5. No Tax on Inputs: In a system of multi-stage production, output at a particular stage of production is input for the next stage. Since at this stage consumption has not taken place, VAT is not collected on inputs. Since VAT operates under a system of tax-credit and rebates, no tax is collected in real sense of the term until the commodity reaches its final destination of consumption.

Broad Advantages of VAT: A few broad advantages of VAT are enumerated as under[12]:

1. It has flexibility of generating large and buoyant revenues.
2. It can be designed to be neutral.
3. It eliminates cascading and hence no tax-induced distortion in favour or against vertical integration.

---

12. Purohit, Mahesh, *op. cit.*, p. 11. and Raja Chelliah, et al., "Introduction to Value Added Tax" in Amaresh Bagchi (ed.), *Readings in Public Finance* , *op. cit.*, p. 227.

The need for vertical integration is dictated only by the market forces or technical consideration and not by the tax structure.

4. It tends to lessen incentive for evasion, as tax does not concentrate the impact on any given level.
5. Tax burden is transparent.
6. Zero rating of tax on exports is easy.
7. No loss of revenue due to a spreading of the base.
8. Since all stages of production and distribution are subject to tax, this form of taxing avoids the problem of undervaluing without introducing cascading.
9. From the point of view of the exchequer, another interesting feature of VAT is its stability as a source of revenue. Owing to the fact that consumption is more stable than income, VAT provides a very stable source of revenue.

Economic Effects of VAT

It is fact universally recognized that taxes do not just provide revenue to the government; they also interfere with the decisions of economic units and affect the level of economic activities in a significant way. As in case of other direct and indirect taxes, the effects of VAT too are felt at different levels of economic activity. VAT influences several macro-economic variables such as savings, investment, employment, distribution, prices and efficiency of resources. VAT affects some of them directly and some others indirectly. A brief discussion follows as under:

Price Effect: The effect of VAT on prices is significant and direct. The effect, however, depends upon whether VAT is a new levy or simply a replacement for the existing tax(es). If VAT is introduced as a replacement of existing commodity taxes then the analysis must consider the effects of reduction in prices due to the abolition of the existing taxes. At the same time, it should take into account the price increase due to introduction VAT. In general, as in the case of other commodity-based taxes, the effect of VAT should be considered in the context of elasticity of demand and supply of a commodity on which VAT is imposed.

Under normal circumstances, VAT is fully shifted forward because traders wish to maintain their level of profit by shifting VAT forward. All traders will initially bear the tax and compliance costs but recoup them in due course. The overall experience suggests that the tax is not inflationary.[13]

Distributional Effects: The distributional effect, however, depends upon the possibility of shifting of VAT. Normally, firms shift the VAT forward. In this case, one has to find out as who are the ultimate users of *vated* commodity, i.e., a commodity on which VAT is imposed. What is their income-consumption group? Since, countrywide there are only one or two rates of VAT and since there are numerous income-consumption groups, it would definitely have a conflicting impact on different income-consumption groups. It has no or minimal impact on high income groups whereas consumers belonging to low and limited income groups are hit hard. Their wage package is generally not flexible enough to take into account a rise in prices because of VAT.

The hardship in above-mentioned problem, largely, can be minimized by a classification of commodities into different groups such basic goods, comforts and luxuries and then vary the VAT rates accordingly. This is done normally; however, any such classification is mainly superficial. This cuts into its simplicity argument where it is maintained that not many rates are required.

The distributional effect of any tax, let alone VAT, depends also upon the possibility of its evasion. The VAT, however, in comparison to other forms of sales tax, stands the test of a proper administration because it involves a self-policing mechanism. The producer/buyer of a *vated* commodity can minimize his own liability by following a strict invoicing so that he can himself claim tax credit.

The distributional impact of VAT could also be understood in the context of backward shifting of VAT. This phenomenon

13. Ahuja, Astha, *op. cit.*, p. 15.

is rare in practice yet possible theoretically. In a monopsony type of market for a factor or input, the VAT can be shifted backward having its own distributional impact.

Finally, it can be mentioned here that the ultimate distributional effect of a VAT should be studied in the context of distributional impact of public expenditure. The tool of public expenditure greatly affects redistributive process. The extent to which the VAT generates sufficient revenue and to the extent these resources are efficiently used, the distributional impact of VAT would be favourable.

Optimal Taxation and Value Added Tax

The literature on optimal taxation has pointed out that a necessary condition for taxes to be designed optimally is to have no tax on inputs going into production. Since VAT avoids tax on inputs and it offers a possibility of tax credit, it is eminently suitable for adoption in an optimal tax structure.

Some Arguments Against VAT

Broadly speaking, VAT is opposed on the following grounds[14]:

1. VAT is more complicated than a simple cascading first point tax. The taxpayer has to keep accounts not only of sales but also of purchases and tax paid on those purchases. Since the tax liability will be based not merely on the value of the total turnover but also on the tax paid on the inputs, there is more administrative work involved. Thus, it is argued that for both taxpayers and administrators, VAT is a more difficult tax to operate.

2. It has been argued that the introduction of VAT would cause some inflation. This argument has been used particularly in countries where there was no general sales tax but only a few excises.

3. VAT has been criticized as a regressive tax. This is possible when VAT is levied at a single rate with no exemptions.

The arguments as mentioned above are not well founded. Regarding the necessity of keeping records, it can be said that

14. Chelliah, Raja, *op. cit.*, p. 279.

records are to be kept, preserved and produced before the tax authorities as and when necessary even for a single point sales tax. It is, however, true that more accounting is needed under VAT. As against this, since there will be only a few rates, at the most two or three; very few exemptions and dealers above the threshold only will pay this tax, in a way VAT is very simple to administer and easy to comply with. Regarding inflationary potential it can be said, as in case of other commodity taxes, if the government is deliberately using VAT as a means of raising revenue in a rational manner, there will be some increase in prices. A certain degree of inflation is inevitable particularly in developing countries. Nevertheless, such inflation cannot be attributed only to the VAT. Regarding regressive nature of VAT, it can be argued that the regressivity could be minimized to some extent by having excises at higher rates on a few goods largely consumed by the richer sections of the society. VAT is no more regressive than any other general tax on commodities and services.

VAT and Evasion

The proponents of VAT claim that evasion under it is difficult and minimal. The credit method ensures cross checking of records of taxpayers through invoices. Buyer firms insist on supplier firms to furnish invoices which help the former to claim tax credit. Thus, evasion appears to be difficult because of self-policing nature of VAT. Despite this, the possibilities of its evasion cannot be ruled out.[15] In fact, VAT provides opportunities for fraud (fictitious claims for refunds) which are not available under other forms of commodity taxation. The methods commonly applied to defraud tax authorities under VAT include, *inter alia*, the following:

1. Use of fake invoices to claim tax credit.
2. Tax credit claims on purchases for personal use.
3. Over reporting of sales of zero-rated goods.
4. Secret deals between buyers and sellers as regards issuance of receipts.
5. Formation of fake companies which sell receipts to traders to enable them to claim tax credit on inputs.

15. Ahuja, Astha, *op. cit.*, p. 11.

In short, VAT is as susceptible to evasion and fraud as any other tax. Efficient tax machinery capable of cross-checking a large number of invoices through an elaborate computer system is a pre-requisite for the successful implementation of VAT. This is precisely what is lacking in an underdeveloped country.[16]

16. *Ibid.*, p. 12.

Tax Reform: Issues and Directions

11

Objective: To examine need for tax reform and study its issues and directions.

Organization: Introduction; defining tax reform; need for tax reform; goals; directions; areas of tax reform.

Introduction

The history of taxation is as old as the history of human civilization because taxes are considered as a cost paid for living in a civilized and organized society. This society not only provides protection to the lives and properties of its members but also helps them in solving their economic problems in the context of scarcity of means on one hand and endless choices on the other. For normal human beings, life away from and without society is simply impossible and, therefore, one cannot but escape from the payment of cost.

The concepts of society and its cost are very old. It was inscribed on a clay tablet dating back to 4500 B.C. that you can manage with king, you can manage with your lord but the man to fear most is tax collector. A long list of complaints against taxes is also equally old. Currently, what more surprising is this fact that the dissatisfaction with the present system is backed by a strong political will to reform the system. This political will has emerged with full force as never before.

Current interest in tax reform has been fueled by almost universal tax reforms in the 1980s. The 1980s was truly a decade of worldwide tax reform. Almost all countries of Western Europe have undergone tax reform during that period. Several developing countries have also undergone or are currently undergoing deep tax reforms. Introduction of VAT is a pointer. It is quite surprising to note that the VAT was almost unknown twenty-five years ago. Now around 130 countries have introduced VAT.

Fiscal theorists and tax administrators hold a unanimous view that there is an urgent need to reform existing tax system because of the following reasons:

1. Complex—difficult to administer and comply with.
2. Inelastic—unresponsive to growth and the changing structure of economic activity.
3. Inefficient—introduce various economic distortions while raising relatively little revenues.
4. Inequitable—treat different individuals and businesses in similar circumstances differently.
5. Unfair—tax administration and enforcement are selective and favour those with the ability to defeat the system.
6. Hybridization—almost all the three major bases [income, consumption and wealth] have lost their pristine purity. It is difficult to say which base is functioning.

The complaints as above are illustrated with the help of following circular Chart 11.1. Everyone is, therefore, for tax reform and naturally there are as many suggestions as there are supporters of it from different corners of the world. In the post-war period, in different countries, we can identify more than one hundred major attempts to reform the tax systems. In our own country India, several such attempts have been made both at the centre and state levels. The appointment of several commissions and committees and their voluminous reports are an unpretentious acknowledgement of an ailing system.

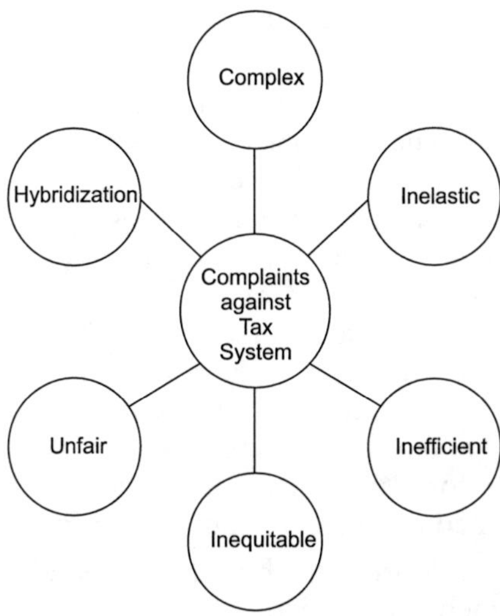

Chart 11.1: Complaints against Tax System

In the context of growing importance of tax reform, an attempt is made here to address four major questions with a special reference to direct taxation: What tax reform means? Why tax reform is required? What should be the goals of tax reform? Which aspects of tax reform have received much attention?

Defining Tax Reform

Tax reform could be defined as a deliberate and a well-calculated attempt on the part of government to minimise complaints against the whole system of taxation. The complaints keep arising because of the failure of the system to achieve the desired goals of equity, efficiency and simplicity. Any debate, be it on the introduction of a new tax, revision of rates of existing taxes, size and number of allowable deductions, changes in exemption limits, revision in the number of tax brackets, etc., centres invariably around the desired goals mentioned above. It may cover increases or decreases in tax rates, brackets or thresholds and changes in the tax base; the introduction of new taxes; abolition of old taxes; and changes in the tax mix. The indexation of major tax bases in view of inflation also constitutes tax reform as does a radical change in administrative practices and procedures.

A quick review of the literature enables us to know that there are three popular notions of tax reform. First, a balanced reduction in government expenditure and thereby level of taxation. In other words, it means downsizing of public sector on one hand and reducing number and rates of taxes on the other. The second notion of tax reform pleads for changing specific features of various taxes such dividend reliefs and partial integration of corporate and personal incomes. This is for the purpose of broadening of tax base on one hand and comprehensive taxation of income on the other. The third notion of tax reform pertains to a switching over of the base from personal income to personal consumption expenditure.

Gillis has developed a methodology of studying tax reform which is extremely useful in the study of different dimensions of tax reform.[1] He is of the view that modifications made on a more or less regular basis whether in underlying laws or administrative rules and procedures could be at best described adjustments and not the reform. Changes in tax system qualify as reform only when these significantly alter the trajectory of the system.

It is to be understood from Gillis notion of tax reform that regular piecemeal adjustments here and there in the system do not fall under the broad definition of a tax reform. Instead, making the system simple to understand and easy to administer, very often these arrangements add to confusions and complexities. Tax reform according to Gillis is neither carried out frequently nor continuously. He is of the view that there could be six options:

A. Reform of the structure or tax administration or reform of tax system.
B. Comprehensive or partial reform.
C. Revenue enhancing, revenue neutral or revenue decreasing reform.
D. Distributionally neutral or redistributing tax reform.

---

1. Gillis, R., *Tax Reform*, Duke University, 1989.

E. Economically neutral or interventionist reform.

F. Contemporaneous, phased or successive reform.

Thus, in the opinion of Gillis, we may envision fifteen different possibilities of tax reform. Taking stock of prevailing fiscal scenario, a country may pursue a reform process that is suitable to its requirements. There are several good works on the subject of tax reform. The reading list could be long and exhaustive as well.[2]

Why Tax Reform is Required?

"Why tax reform is required" is a question which takes us back to the examination of role of taxation as to how it changed with the change in the role of state. Three dominant economic philosophies have shaped the role of state and thereby the character of taxation. Already pointed out earlier, these are (1) Libertarian, (2) Collectivist and (3) Neo-Liberals.[3] In the Table 11.1 an attempt is made to trace implications of the above-mentioned economic philosophies for public finance of which taxation is an integral part.[4]

Table 11.1: Dominant Economic Philosophies and Implications for Public Finance

Libertarian	Collectivist	Neo-Liberal
Minimal public finance	Unrestrained public finance	Restrained public finance
Private spending replaces public spending	Public replaces private spending	Seek additionality for public spending
Minimum burden of taxation	Redistributive taxes for equity	Tax 'bads' not 'goods' for efficiency
Regressive taxes	Progressive taxes	Proportional taxes
Minimal public expenditure	Expansive public expenditure	Restrained public expenditure
Limited public borrowing	Expansive public borrowing	Restrained public borrowing

The attitude of classical economists, identified with libertarian approach, towards the role of government is well

2. Discerning readers may to refer to the works of Nicholas Stern, David Newbery, Ehtisham Ahmad, Vito Tanzi, *et al.*

3. Readers are advised to refer the first chapter of this book.

4. Adopted with modification from Stephen, J. Bailey, *op. cit.*, p. 6.

known.[5] Adam Smith's vision of invisible hand and his notion of government are very clear. He is of the view that the state has three important functions to perform. First, it should protect people from internal violence and external aggression. Second, it should provide justice so as to ensure individuals' liberty. Finally, it should maintain and erect those public institutions and works whose provision is of great advantage to the society and in whose provision, private parties are least interested. Their lack of interest is normally attributed to low rates of return on one hand and long gestation periods on the other.

Other classical economists such as Say, Ricardo, Bastiat and Parnell held still more orthodox view and they assigned a very limited role to the state. Say argued that the very best of all plans of finance is to spend a little and best of all taxes is the one which is least in amount. Ricardo supported Say maintaining that if you want a peaceful government you must reduce the size of budget. "Ricardo evidently found public expenditures so wasteful that he did not feel it necessary to discuss them. He was satisfied to endorse the golden maxim of Say that the very best of all plans of finance is to spend little."[6] Bastiat was still clearer as he remarked that the government cannot have any other function but the legitimate defence of individual rights. He challenged that beyond provision of justice, any intervention from government is a blunder. Parnell declared that every particle of expenditure that was incurred beyond necessity absolutely required for the preservation of social order and for protection against foreign attacks was waste and unjust. It could result in imposition of burdensome and exacting levies on public.

A close examination of statements of above mentioned classical economists makes it clear that their concept of role of government was vastly different from the one being perceived today. They believed in the efficiency of market mechanism in resource allocation. Much significance was attached to the efficiency of productive agents and there wasn't a talk on

5. For further details the reader may refer to first chapter in this book.
6. Musgrave, Richard A., *op. cit.*, p. 68.

allocative and distributive roles of the state. They impressed upon governments to leave money to fructify in the pockets of people instead being extracted through taxation and spent unproductively and even wastefully.

Classical economists succeeded in carving out a limited role for government and therefore the size of public expenditure remained small. Neither many taxes nor high rates were required. All went well till the beginning of depressing conditions of 1930. The Great Depression, which started from U.S. and gradually engulfed whole world, shook the confidence of people, economists and politicians in the non-interventionist role of the state. Thousands of factories were closed and millions of people lost their jobs. In the process, they also lost a hope for their better and decent future. In U.S. and elsewhere, GNP fell sharply, prices and profits nose-dived. Those very people who in the ordinary course of time would not have tolerated any intervention started crying desperately for a help from governments. This contention started gaining more support that market mechanism is not always necessarily efficient and some sort of government regulation is necessary. Emergence of Keynesian economics further consolidated interventionist ideas. Economists trained in Keynesian traditions pleaded for regulating market forces in order to stabilize economic activities. They also pleaded for a progressive transfer of funds from private hands to public coffers for a more socially-oriented spending. Progressive transfer of funds was also desired to minimize uneven income and wealth distribution. As time flew, efficiency consideration was pushed to an inferior position.

Emphasis on stabilization and distribution led to a heavy public spending, huge budgetary deficits and high levels of taxation. Public expenditure as a percentage of GDP increased considerably reflecting an increased role of government. This may be attributed to a number of factors. First, a certain level of government facilitation is required for resource allocation. Second, there is an increased concern for an equitable redistribution of income and wealth. Third, government regulation is desired to maintain economic stability. Finally, during 1950s and 1960s a large number of countries in Asia, Africa and Latin America got independence after centuries of colonial rule. These countries aimed at growing at a fast pace in order to make up the lost time and opportunities.

The above-mentioned factors led to a phenomenal increase in public expenditure. At present, in many developing countries, the situation is such that any talk of a decrease in public expenditure is considered as unwise not because all public expenditure programmes are highly efficient and productive but the parties in power are afraid of losing public support and popular vote. In these countries, expenditure scenario is characterized by a high proportion of interest payments to total expenditure, huge subsidies and phenomenal increase in expenditure on internal and external security.

In the above backdrop, high taxes, both on men and materials, were considered as a convenient means of transferring resources for public spending. At a given point of time, we can observe some sort of relationship between taxation and expenditure levels. Currently, in a large number of developed and developing countries, it is the size of expenditure which is dictating taxation level and not the other way round. In recent decades, allocative and distributive considerations have overshadowed the efficiency argument which was the focal point of discussion on taxation during the classical period and much thereafter. In this way, less attention was paid to the fact that tax progression conflicts with efficiency and that the efficiency costs could be more than the gain in other areas.

Since the beginning of 1980s, complaints against tax system in general and personal income tax in particular started multiplying. This is not to say that the process of income taxation in the past was hassle free. What new today is the convergence of perceptions of economists and their political bosses on efficiency losses. They are now maintaining that a system of high rates, growing expenditure, huge budgetary deficits and stifling intervention has done more damage than good. In this context, the neo-liberals have heavily attacked "cradle-to-grave" approach of modern welfare governments.

Previously, complaints were directed against either tax rates or frequent changes in fatuous tax laws accommodating tax concessions, deductions and exemptions, etc. At present, these complaints are not against any one aspect but the whole system is considered as an impediment to economic growth, factor productivity, private enterprise and capital formation. The U.S. Treasury Report pointed out that the system is complex and inequitable. It reduces economic incentives, hampers economic growth and is perceived to be so unfair that taxpayers' morale and voluntary compliance have been seriously undermined.[7] These observations support Seligman who almost 80 years ago gave a warning which was unfortunately ignored because of obsession with the notion that of all taxes, the personal income tax is fairer of them all. He wrote that even if the income tax were fairer of all taxes which is not necessarily true, the decision as to whether this fairness, which is predicted of it in abstract, would ensure in actual practice. It is notorious, however, that of all taxes the income tax is perhaps most difficult to assess with scrupulous justice and accuracy so that what is conceived as just results in crass injustice.[8]

Suspicion against the System

The growing suspicion against the whole system of taxation was due to several developments. First, persistent price rise distorted tax bases and created measurement problems. Secondly, there is growing recognition that high marginal tax rates have greatly damaged the notion of horizontal equity. Thirdly, high marginal rates have over the years contributed to a large scale tax evasion and rapid expansion of underground economic activities. Since these activities fall outside the fiscal net, in the long run, these make fiscal tools ineffective. Finally, it is getting increasingly realized that high taxes inhibit capital formation and growth. In the past, different taxes were imposed as a means of raising

7. The U.S. Treasury Report, Washington D.C., 1984.
8. For a classical treatment of this topic one may refer to Edwin R. Seligman's *Progressive Taxation in Theory and Practice* 2nd Edition, Princeton University Press, Princeton, N.J., 1908.

revenue and essentially these were not used for non-revenue purposes as being done today. A number of authors have emphasized that the process of revenue generation should not suppress or adversely affect productive agents which carry the burden of lifting and then sustaining economy on desired growth path.

In brief, during 1980s, it was increasingly realized that the tax systems all over the world have become unfair, inefficient and hopelessly complicated. These checked growth and prevented workers and economy from reaching to their full potential. Tax reform was, therefore, considered as a need of the hour and men in-charge of public policy and affairs were asked to be pragmatic.

Objectives of Tax Reform

In the context of the above discussion, the following broad objectives of tax reform may be set[9]:

1. Simplicity: The tax reform should aim at making the tax system simple enough to enable taxpayers to understand the rules and comply with them correctly and cost effectively. Simplicity reduces the number of errors, improves compliance and increases respect for the reform. Although the truly simple tax system may not be possible, the level of complexity should be appropriate for the taxpayers or the transactions involved. Simplicity is the basis for achieving many of the remaining tax policy goals, including transparency, minimizing non-compliance, cost-effective collection, and payment convenience. The less complex a tax system is, the better taxpayers are able to anticipate the tax consequences of their economic choices.

2. Fairness: The tax reform should intend to achieve fairness which is usually evaluated by looking at the horizontal and vertical equity. Horizontal equity means that taxpayers with equal abilities should pay the same amount of tax. Vertical equity means that taxpayers with a greater ability to

9. American Institute of Certified Public Accountants, Inc., *Understanding Tax Reform: A Guide to 21st Century Alternatives*, New York, September, 2005, pp. 10-13.

pay should pay more tax. Defining and achieving equity is a matter for political, social and economic debate.

3. Economic Growth and Efficiency: The tax reform process desires that the tax system should not impede or reduce an economy's productive capacity. A tax system should encourage economic growth, capital formation and international competitiveness. In general, tax system should not favour one industry or type of investment at the expense of others. By recognizing the economic effects of choosing what to tax and at what rate, policy-makers can work towards intended economic results and avoid unintended consequences.

4. Neutrality: The process of tax reform favours that tax considerations should have the smallest possible effect on a taxpayer's economic decisions about whether or how to carry out a particular transaction. A neutral tax system neither encourages nor discourages taxpayers from engaging in certain activities. A completely neutral tax system is unlikely. Although the primary purpose of a tax system is to raise revenue, tax law is often purposefully used to influence taxpayer behaviour. However, within the system, the system should be neutral when determining how to measure income, the appropriate tax rate and taxpayers ability to pay.

5. Transparency: Tax reform intends to achieve transparency which signifies that the taxpayers should know that a tax exists and how and when it is imposed upon them and others. Transparency enables taxpayers to know the true cost of transactions and to better understand the impact of the tax system. Transparency is an important partner to tax simplification because complex provisions make it more difficult for taxpayers to assess whether and when they will be taxed.

6. Minimizing Non-compliance: Tax reform intends to minimize non-compliance. The "tax gap" between the amount of tax owed and the amount collected can be minimized by increasing the ease of compliance, decreasing the incentive to avoid compliance and using appropriate procedural rules and enforcement measures. Generally, a balance must be struck among the desired level of compliance and the costs and intrusiveness of enforcement.

7. Cost-Effective Collection: The process of tax reform favours that the costs to collect a tax should be kept to a minimum for both the government and taxpayers. Consideration should be given both to the number of revenue officers needed to administer the tax and to the compliance costs for taxpayers. This principle is closely related to the principle of simplicity.

8. Impact on Government Revenues: The government should be able to determine, with reasonable certainty, the amount and timing of tax collections. Policy-makers need to predictably and reliably achieve a desired level of revenue within a reasonable range. Generally, a tax system that combines a variety of tax sources will permit a more stable source of revenue for example, rising unemployment leads to reduced income tax collections but property taxes and sales taxes might be less affected, thereby total revenue would be less volatile than if the government solely relied on an income tax.

9. Certainty: Taxpayers need to be able to calculate their tax liabilities. Tax rules should clearly specify how to determine the amount of tax owed and when and how the tax must be paid. Uncertainty results if taxpayers have difficulty in measuring the tax base, determining the applicable tax rate or anticipating the tax consequences of a transaction. When taxpayers lack confidence that they know (1) what their tax obligations are; (2) whether their calculations are correct; and (3) if their returns are properly filed, compliance rates fall and collection costs rise.

10. Payment Convenience: The tax reform favours that the payment of tax should be convenient to the taxpayers. This facilitates compliance. Here the important considerations are: is it better to collect the tax from employer or employee? From wholesaler or retailer or consumer? Should the tax be collected annually, quarterly, monthly or weekly?

Thrust Areas of Tax Reform

Achieving objectives as mentioned above means creating a simpler, fairer and more economically efficient tax system. Our next issue is to examine the major areas of tax reform.

A cursory survey of tax reform process across the globe brings to our notice three thrust areas:

First, a reduction in tax rates in general and top marginal rates in particular.

Second, broadening of tax bases.

Third, a reduction in the number of tax brackets.

A universal complaint against the present system was that tax rates, particularly income tax rates, were fairly high. Several countries during 1950s and 1960s followed a policy of soaking rich, totally ignoring the fact that rich contribute more towards capital formation and thereby enterprise and growth. While growth of private sector was curbed, the public sector was managed by such managers who were least bothered about the financial accountability. After all it was not their money or stock at the stake.

In order to quench public sector thirst for more funds, governments, on one hand, raised tax rates and on the other, private sector was squeezed. Tax rates reached to such heights that they were regarded as confiscatory penalizing every additional unit of work done and income earned. In the process, faith and zeal of highly productive economic agents were lost. Cumulative tax burden made dishonesty more rewarding than integrity and hard work.

The Laffer Curve has more meaningfully explained the impact of high tax rates. Even though the validity of Laffer Curve can be questioned, yet it has more passionately demonstrated income and substitution effects than several recent studies combined together. The Laffer Curve is more meaningful, appealing and easy to digest than several highly mathematical analyses of adverse impact of high income tax rates.

Arthur Laffer was an advisor to President Reagan in the early 1980s. The idea is clear: "at both extremes of taxation—

zero per cent and one-hundred per cent", the government collects no revenue. At one extreme, a 0 per cent tax rate means the government's revenue is, of course, zero. At the other, where there is a 100 per cent tax rate, the government collects zero revenue because (in a "Rational" economic model) taxpayers have no incentive to work or they avoid taxes, and the government collects 100 per cent of nothing. Somewhere between 0 per cent and 100 per cent, therefore, lies a tax rate that will maximize revenue. This is illustrated by the Laffer curve:

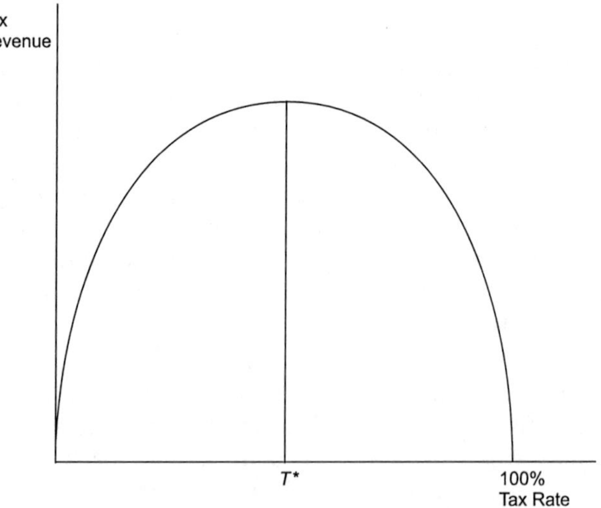

Fig. 11.1: Relation between Tax Rate and Revenue—Laffer Curve

T^* represents the optimum tax rate where the maximum amount of tax revenue can be collected. Laffer and other right-wing economists used the curve to argue that taxes were currently too high and should therefore be reduced to encourage incentives and harder work (a supply-side policy).[10] Others argue that we are already well to the left of T^*. It justifies tax cuts and intends to show that government can maximize revenue by setting a tax rate at the peak of this curve.

10. www.bized.ac.uk/economy/virtuallibrary.

Laffer reportedly sketched the curve on a napkin to illustrate the concept, which immediately caught the imaginations of people at large. Laffer himself professes no recollection of this napkin, but writes, "I used the so-called Laffer Curve all the time in my classes and with anyone else who would listen to me."[11] The fact, most surprising as well as most neglected, is that Laffer also does not claim to have invented the concept. He attributes it to 14th century scholar Ibn-Khuldun.[12]

Authorities are now more concerned about the adverse effects of a highly progressive rate structure. They have also taken a very serious note of a large scale tax evasion. During the last two decades, several countries have reduced top marginal rates. These are at present at least two to three times lower than before. The driving force behind such a reduction is the basic economic insight that high marginal tax rates have disproportionately large burdens. The Table 11.2 contains information regarding reduction in top rates of income in selected OECD countries:

Table 11.2: Top Rates of Central Government Personal Income Tax in Selected OECD Countries

Country	1976	1986	1992	Percentage points reduction: 1976 figure minus 1992 figure
Australia	65	57	48	17
Austria	62	62	50	12
Canada	43	34	29	14
Finland	51	51	39	12
France	60	65	57	3
Germany	56	56	53	3
Ireland	77	58	52	25
Italy	72	62	50	22
Japan	75	70	50	25
Netherlands	72	72	60	12
New Zealand	60	57	33	27
Norway	48	40	13	35
Sweden	57	50	20	27
UK	83	60	40	43
USA	70	50	31	39
Unweighted average	63.4	56.3	41.7	21.7

Source: Various OECD publications.

11. www.bized.ac.uk/economy/virtuallibrary.
12. *Ibid.*

The second major area of tax reform is the broadening of tax base. This is being done by eliminating the number of and reducing size of several tax concessions, allowable deductions and exemptions. A reduction in tax rates coupled with the broadening of tax base, as the popular argument develops, enables tax authorities to collect the same amount of revenue or even more. This line has gained a considerable acceptance that mere high tax rates do not necessarily ensure more revenue but a broad base is also equally important. The practice so far has been that on one hand high tax rates were administered on the other a whole plethora of deductions was allowed leading to steady erosion in the tax base itself.

Reducing number of tax brackets is the third major area of tax reform. A few tax brackets are advocated on simplicity ground. Several brackets would be required when tax rates are many because each bracket must necessarily be tagged to a particular rate band. It, therefore, follows that a few brackets are administered when rate bands are limited in number. Currently, this perception is more popular that if the first bracket is very wide, then for all practical purposes, a large number of taxpayers will be facing what for them becomes a *de facto* proportional income tax with the obvious efficiency advantages. In recent times, the Japanese tax reform has gone so far as to make the size of first tax bracket wide enough to accommodate a large number of income taxpayers over their entire career.

The process of tax reform in United Kingdom began in the year 1979 when Conservative Party came to power. It described the tax system left by the previous Labour Government as confiscatory and stifling economic growth. It alleged that in order to finance public sector, the Labour Government introduced a number of new taxes as well as raising the rate of existing taxes. These distorted personal, business and investment decisions of individuals and companies. Economic activity got depressed. The first threshold of personal income tax was too low drawing into tax net many who should not have been there. The Conservatives, therefore, viewed tax reform as an urgent necessity. Its thrust was on reducing tax burden, elimination of number of outdated and distortionary exemptions and special reliefs. By doing so, it was expected to achieve advantages of a broad tax base with low rates; improve incentives and encourage people to work more; encourage companies to raise resources more easily and make the tax system both simple to understand and easy to administer. With these specific considerations, tax threshold was raised by 20 per cent, the number of brackets was reduced from thirteen to six and income tax rates at the top were reduced by more than one third. Corporate tax rates were reduced from 52 per cent to 35 per cent and for smaller companies, from 42 per cent to 32 per cent.

In U.S., coming under the strong demonstration effect of Laffer Curve, the Regan Administration (1980-88) took some bold decisions. The Tax Reform Act sharply reduced the number of tax brackets from fifteen to two. Tax base was broadened by eliminating a number of deductions. Highest marginal income tax rates were reduced from 50 per cent to 28 per cent, corporate income tax rate was reduced from 46 per cent to 34 per cent.

Trends akin to the above are noticeable in several other countries including India. Here we find a reduction in personal income tax rates, at the top it is at present 30 per cent. In 1960s and 1970s, there were more than a dozen tax brackets and corresponding rates. Now there are only three. In India, the process of lowering personal income tax rates and reducing the number of brackets began more than two decades ago. In 1971-72, the highest marginal tax rate was 97.5 per cent. This rate was reduced to 75 per cent in 1974-75 and to 60 per cent in 1976-77 and to 55 per cent in 1985-86. This is clear from the Tables 11.3 and 11.4.

Table 11.3: Tax Rates in India

Year	Lowest Rate	Highest Rate
1968-69 to 1969-70	5	75
1970-71 to 1973-74	11	93.5
1974-75	13.2	77
1980-81	15	66

(Contd.)

Year	Lowest Rate	Highest Rate
1985-86	25	50
1990-91	20	56
1991-92	20	56
1995-96	20	40
1997-98	10	30
1998-99	10	30
1999-00	10	33
2000-01	10	35
2001-02	10	30
2002-03	10	30
2003-04	10	30
2005-06	10	30

Table 11.4: Number of Slabs

(Rs. '000)

Year	No. of Slabs	Lowest Slab	Highest Slab
1975-76	8	6-10	70-
1976-77	7	8-15	75-
1977-78 to 1981-82	8	8-15	100-
1982-83	6	15-25	100-
1983-84	8	15-25	100-
1984-85	9	15-25	100-
1985-86 to 1986-87	8	15-25	100-
1987-88 to 1990-91	4	18-25	100-
1991-92 to 1992-93	4	22-30	100-
1993-94	3	28-50	100-
1995-96	3	40-50	120-
1997-98	3	40-50	150-
2004-05	3	50-60	150-
2005-06	3	100-150	250-
2007-08	3	100-150	250-

The corporate income tax rate also stands reduced. Efforts are made to improve compliance by making the return filing process simple one.

In conclusion, it can be said that at present, several economists and their political bosses have realized the efficiency losses on account of administering a regime of high tax rates. They do not deny the importance of taxes as a tool of raising revenue, they, however, are questioning validity of high tax rates.[13] Tax bases are being broadened, the number of brackets is getting smaller and width of tax brackets getting larger. In many countries, practical experience has demonstrated that there was no revenue loss on account of lowering of tax rates. On the contrary, revenue collections surged. Now more and more economic activities are getting recorded and voluntary compliance has increased. Governments in several countries have succeeded in conveying this message to their people that many in small proportion, and not a few in large proportions, should contribute to the exchequer for a larger benefit of all.

13. For efficiency loss the reader may refer to the lecture on 'Excess Burden of Taxation' in this volume.

Towards Goods and Services Tax

12

Objective: To study the concept and working of Goods and Services Tax (GST).

Organization: The idea of consumption basket; occupational changes; present status of occupational structure in India; need for GST; equity argument; what is GST; introduction in India and elsewhere; the working of GST; requirements of GST.

The Idea of Consumption Basket

The idea of consumption-basket is well known to the students of economics. Issues such as getting hold of consumption basket, its extension and retention dominate any discussion on consumer behaviour. The welfare level of an individual consumer is closely linked to the size and nature of consumption basket.

At any given point of time, the consumption-basket comprises of two major constituents namely goods and services. It should be noted here that at the lower end of income the proportion of goods happens to be higher than services and at the higher end of income the proportion of services rises. Individuals at the higher end of income are more conscious of different types of goods and services.

From the viewpoint of taxation, the approach of tax authorities so far was partial. It is in the sense that only one constituent of consumption-basket, i.e., goods were taxed while services, for all practical purposes, were ignored. They have now realised that this approach is detrimental in the context of additional resource mobilisation effort. Since a worldwide tendency is observed in the rapid expansion of services, these provide a strong basis for taxation. There are two aspects of services, one being the use of services and the other being the provision of service. In the interest of additional resource mobilisation, either of the two should be taxed. Viewed from the administrative viewpoint, the scale tilts in the favour of latter.

Occupational Changes

Almost all developed and developing countries of the world have experienced changes in occupational structure where a uniform pattern of change can be noticed. Over the decades, the size and contribution of primary sector to the GDP has declined and that of tertiary sector, comprising of different types of services, has increased. British economy before the advent of industrial revolution, American economy before Civil War and Japanese economy before Meiji Restoration, were all agricultural. Now, in these economies, agriculture has lost the prime position which it once enjoyed. Economists such as Colin Clark and A.G.B. Fisher argue that there is a distinct relationship between economic development and changes in occupational structure, both affecting each other during the course of time. Table 12.1 sheds light on the relative changes and helps us to understand the growing importance of services sector.

Table 12.1: Output and Employment Share in Selected Developed and Developing Countries (2002)

Country	Shares in Output (%)			Shares in Employment (%)		
	Agriculture	Industry	Services	Agriculture	Industry	Services
U.K.	1	26	73	1	25	74
U.S.	2	23	75	2	24	74
France	2	22	76	3	25	72
Japan	1	31	68	5	31	64

(Contd.)

Germany	1	30	69	3	33	64
Italy	3	29	69	5	32	63
Australia	4	26	69	5	21	74
Korea	3	35	62	10	28	62
Malaysia	10	49	42	18	32	50
China	13	46	41	47	22	31
Indonesia	17	44	40	44	17	39
India	22	27	51	61	17	22

Source: World Bank 2004, *World Development Indicators.*

From Table 12.1 it is clear that in almost all developed and industrialised countries of the world the contribution of services sector is either more than or very close to seventy per cent. Similar trend can be noticed in the employment shares. In case of developing countries such as Korea, Malaysia, China, Indonesia and India the share of services is significant. As the time is passing by, the share of services sector is improving further.

Present Status of Occupational Structure in India

It can be especially noted with reference to India that in the recent decades, there is a marked shift in occupational structure in favour of services sector. Table 12.2 contains data pertaining to changes in inter-sectoral composition of GDP in India.

Table 12.2: Changes in Inter-Sectoral Composition of GDP in India

(in per cent)

Year	Share in GDP		
	Agriculture	Industry	Services
1980-81	38.1	20.9	41.0
1984-85	35.9	22.9	41.1
1990-91	30.9	28.4	43.7
1995-96	26.0	26.7	47.0
1996-97	28.0	22.0	49.9
1997-98	26.4	22.3	51.2
1998-99	26.8	22.0	51.2

(Contd.)

2001-02	24.4	19.3	56.3
2002-03	21.9	19.9	58.3
2003-04	22.2	19.5	58.3
2004-05	20.8	19.5	59.7
2005-06	19.7	19.5	60.9

Source: Report on Currency and Finance, various volumes.

It is, thus, clear from the above Table 12.2 that over the years the share of agriculture in GDP has declined. This decline is significant. It was 38.1 per cent in 1980-81, which came down to 19.7 per cent in 2005-06. The share of industry too has declined but this decline is insignificant as compared to agriculture. As against these declines, the share of services has increased significantly. It has increased from 41 per cent in 1980-81 to 60.9 per cent in 2005-06. These changes in inter-sectoral composition of GDP are in line with the development experience, as noted in the preceding Table 12.1.

The Need for Goods and Services Tax

All over the world, economists and policy-makers have noted changes in inter-sectoral composition of GDP and the emergence of services sector as a dominant component of GDP. Accordingly, they have started arguing that the services sector should also bear a good share of tax burden. In India, the Tax Reform Committee [1991] recommended introduction of tax on services. It suggested, to begin with, taxation of advertising, non-life insurance, services of stockbrokers and telephone services. In 1994-95 Budget Speech, the then Finance Minister observed: "There is no sound reason for exempting services from taxation when goods are taxed and many countries treat goods and services alike for tax purpose."

In this context, it is also very appropriate to note the observations made Reserve Bank of India in its annual *Report on Currency and Finance* (1998-99): "The tax revenue from the agricultural sector being negligible, the industrial sector continues to constitute the only principal tax base though it has suffered a reduction in the share of GDP over the period. Despite the fact that the services sector has shown substantial buoyancy, its contribution to the exchequer is not significant in relation to its sizeable share in GDP. Thus, in order to impart buoyancy to the revenue receipts and to provide consistency and equity in the tax structure *vis-à-vis* the composition of income, it is imperative to bring major part of services sector under the tax net."

The goods and service tax (GST) is proposed to be a comprehensive indirect tax levy on manufacture, sale and consumption of goods as well as services both at a national and state levels. Integration of goods and services taxation would give India a world class tax system and improve tax collections. It would end the long-standing distortions of differential treatments of manufacturing and service sector. The introduction of goods and services tax will lead to the abolition of taxes such as octroi, Central sales tax, State level sales tax, entry tax, stamp duty, telecom licence fees, turnover tax, tax on consumption or sale of electricity, taxes on transportation of goods and services, and eliminate the cascading effects of multiple layers of taxation. GST will facilitate seamless credit across the entire supply chain and across all states under a common tax base.

The indirect tax system in India is currently mired in multi-layered taxes—such as excise duty, octroi, CST, value added tax (VAT) and service tax among others—levied by the Centre and state governments. These cause distortions in the tax regime and lead to huge leakages. Once implemented, GST is expected to remove these distortions, as most of these taxes would be replaced by it. About 150 countries across the world have introduced GST in one form or the other. The GST rate in various countries ranges from as low as 5 per cent in Taiwan to as high as 25 per cent in Denmark. To sustain growth performance of Indian economy over a longer period, we need to complete the process of indirect tax reforms leading to a comprehensive goods and services tax (GST).

The Argument of Equity

As pointed out above the consumption-basket comprises of goods and services. The practice prevalent so far is to tax goods only. Strictly, from the equity viewpoint, both goods and services should be taxed. There will be a distortion in the relative prices of goods and services when goods only are taxed and services are excluded. This also leads to distortion in the allocation of resources.

From the viewpoint of comprehensive taxation, it can be said that the exclusion of services narrows the tax base. A narrow tax base has its own economic costs. If it is required to raise a given amount revenue, the tax rate on goods needs to be high. The inclusion of services broadens tax base and a broad tax base has its own economic advantages. It enables tax authorities to collect a given amount of revenue with low rates. Thus, in the context of (1) rapidly changing occupational structure, (2) need to mobilise additional revenue to finance ever-increasing public expenditure, and (3) in the interest of equity, it is necessary to bring the provision of services into the tax net.

The Introduction of GST in India and Elsewhere

The idea of a broad-based consumption tax was first proposed by then Australian federal treasurer Paul Keating at the 1985 Tax Summit but was dropped at the behest of then Labour Prime Minister Bob Hawke after pressure from the ACTU, welfare groups and business. It was introduced by the Howard Government on 1 July 2000, replacing the previous Federal wholesale sales tax system and designed to phase out a number of various State and Territory Government taxes, duties and levies such as banking taxes and stamp duty. In Canada despite the opposition, the tax came into force on January 1, 1991.

In the context of additional resource mobilisation, consistent rise in the share of services sector and realisation all over the world that the services could be another base for taxation a modest attempt was made in India in the year 1994-95. The then Union Finance Minister introduced a 5 per cent services tax on three services namely telephone services, non-life insurance services and services of stock brokers. Since then the number of services is increasing as more and more services are being added to the list of taxable services. Table 12.3 sheds light on the number of taxable services and assessees starting from the year of introduction [1994-95].

Table 12.3: Number of Services and Number of Assessees

Year	Number of Services	Number of Assessees
1994-95	03	3943
1995-96	03	4866
1996-97	06	13982
1997-98	15	45991
1998-99	26	107479
1999-00	26	115495
2000-01	26	122326
2001-02	41	187577
2002-03	52	232048
2003-04	60	403856
2004-05	75	740267
2005-06	84	805591
2006-07	99	–
2007-08	104	–

Source: Budget Documents.

The Union Finance Minister in his budget speech [2006] indicated that the country will have Goods and Service Tax (GST) regime in 2010. With successful introduction of VAT in almost all the states and continuous increase in number of services under the service tax net, nobody should have any doubt of the Finance Minister's seriousness about GST. The Finance Minister in his 2006 Budget speech said: "It is my sense that there is a large consensus that the country should move towards a National Level Goods and Service Tax (GST) that should be shared between the Centre and the States. I propose that we set April 1, 2010 as the date of introducing GST. World over, Goods and Services attract the same rate of Tax. This is the foundation of GST. People must get used to the idea of a GST. We must progressively converge the service tax rate and Cenvat rate." The introduction of GST will help India achieve economies of scale by becoming a common market, and help India score in the global market for labour-intensive manufacturing.

In the recent budget of 2009-10 the government announced the final roadmap for implementing a countrywide goods and services tax (GST) from April 1, 2010. It is hailed one of the most comprehensive tax reforms initiatives in independent India. The Union Finance Minister said in his 2009-10 budget speech: "Tax reform, like all reforms, is a process and not an event. We have accelerated the process for the smooth introduction of GST with effect from April 1, 2010." The broad contour of the GST Model is that it will be a dual GST comprising of a Central GST and a State GST. The Centre and the States will each legislate, levy and administer the Central GST and State GST, respectively. The Central Government will play a catalytic role to facilitate the introduction of GST by 1st April, 2010 after due consultations with all stakeholders.

What is Goods and Services Tax

Goods and Service Tax is a tax on goods and services, which is leviable at each point of sale or provision of service, in which at the time of sale of goods or providing the services the seller or service provider can claim the input credit of tax which he has paid while purchasing the goods or procuring the service. On most of the goods and services the rate of tax remains the same but as per the necessity of the nation some goods or services can be declared as "exempted" or "Zero rated". The whole system is developed in such a way that it avoids the cascading effect and the final consumer bears the burden of all the tax. Generally, in such a system exports are zero rated and all the taxes paid while purchasing and manufacturing the goods including the taxes paid on raw material and services are returned to the exporter to make the exports competitive.

The sellers or service providers collect the tax from their customer, who may or may not be the ultimate customer, and before depositing the same to the exchequer, they deduct the tax they have already paid. This is simply very similar to VAT which is at present applicable in most of the states and can be termed as National level VAT on Goods and Services with only one difference that in this system not only goods but also services are involved and the rate of tax on goods and services are generally the same.

Economic and Social Effects of the GST

Critics have argued that the GST is a regressive tax, which has a more pronounced effect on lower income earners, meaning that the tax consumes a higher proportion of their income, compared to those earning large incomes. This criticism of GST is not always correct and valid. Certain goods and services are favourably treated, as under VAT, thereby avoiding any chance of adverse impact on low income consumers. Further, its economic effect would be very much similar to that of VAT. GST is inflationary if it is an additional levy. It is non-inflationary to the extent it replaces existing taxes on goods and services.

The Working of GST

The following aspects need to be considered here[1]:

A. **Charging the Tax:** The dealers registered under GST (Manufacturers, Wholesalers and Retailers and Service Providers) are required to charge GST at the specified rate of tax on goods and services that they supply to customers. The GST payable is included in the price paid by the buyers of the goods and services.

B. **Getting Credit of GST:** If the seller of goods or services is a registered dealer (Manufacturers,

1. Halakhandi, Sudhir, "Goods and Services Tax: An Introductory Study", *Chartered Accountant,* April, 2007. For a very thorough study one may also refer to R. Kavita Rao "Goods and Services Tax for India", Working Paper 57, November 2008, National Institute of Public Finance and Policy, New Delhi.

Wholesalers and Retailers and Service Providers), he will normally be able to claim a credit for the amount of GST he has paid, provided he holds a proper tax invoice. This "input tax credit" is set off against any GST (Output), which the dealer charges on goods and services, which he supplies, to his customers.

C. **Ultimate Burden of Tax on Last Customer:** The net effect is that dealers pay GST but get a credit for it. This means that they act essentially as collecting agents for the Government. The ultimate burden of the tax falls on the last and final consumer of the goods and services, as this person gets no credit for the GST paid by him to his sellers or service providers.

D. **Registration:** Dealers will have to register for GST. These dealers will include the suppliers, manufacturers, service providers, wholesalers and retailers. If a dealer is not registered, he normally cannot charge GST and cannot claim credit for the GST he pays and further cannot issue a tax invoice.

E. **Tax Period:** The tax period will have to be decided by the respective law and normally it is monthly and/or quarterly. On a particular tax period, which is applicable to the dealer concerned, the dealer has to deposit the tax if his output credit is more than the input credit after considering the opening balance, if any, of the input credit.

F. **Refunds:** If for a tax period the input credit of a dealer is more than the output credit then he is eligible for refund subject to the provisions of law applicable in this respect. The excess may be carried forward to next period or may be refunded immediately depending upon the provision of law.

G. **Exempted Goods and Services:** Certain goods and services may be declared as exempted goods and services and in that case the input credit cannot be claimed on the GST paid for purchasing the raw material in this respect or GST paid on services used for providing such goods and services.

H. **Zero Rated Goods and Services:** Generally, export of goods and services are zero-rated and in that case the GST paid by the exporters of these goods and services is refunded. This is the basic difference between Zero rated goods and services and exempted goods and services.

GST and Present System of VAT

In principle, there is no difference between present tax structure under VAT and GST as far as the tax on goods is concerned because GST is also a form of VAT on Goods and services. Here at present the sales tax, with an exception of CST, is a VAT system and in case of service tax the system also has the Cenvat credit system hence both sales tax and service tax are under VAT system in our country. At present the goods and services are taxed separately but in GST the difference will be vanished. The overall system of GST is very much similar to the VAT, which can be considered as first step towards GST.

When we have VAT in almost the whole country and the system of central excise and service tax is well equipped with the Cenvat credit, then why is there a need of GST? Well, this is needed to match the international phenomenon. It is needed to reduce the burden of Central excise. The introduction of GST will certainly change the Federal system of Governance in our country in which states also have the right to collect taxes on goods. A national level GST would be ideal on the ground of simplicity. It would minimise compliance cost to the taxpayers as they will be required to deal with only one tax agency. It would also minimize tax induced distortions.

Requirements for GST

The immediate requirements in the introduction of GST may be identified as under:

1. Constitutional and legal changes. States should also have concurrent powers to tax services.

2. The development of the IT systems. The Tax Information Network (TIN) system, built by NSDL, is the right foundation for implementing the GST.
3. The consolidating of Central Excise, the Central Service Tax and VAT on imports (i.e. CVD) into a single tax called the Central GST.
4. The political effort of interacting with the states. It may involve the question of revenue sharing. The fairest formulation would place the entire GST collection into the hands of the Finance Commission for sharing with States. Calculations and fiscal scenarios must be made, and discussed with State finance ministers, in order to arrive at an agreement.
5. There may be a clash of interest of the Centre with the states hence the task will not be that easy. Since sales taxes contribute more than 60 per cent of states' own revenues, the states would not give up their tax powers without bargaining.
6. Administrative efforts at the state level particularly computerisation of tax system.

The Performance So Far

We know it very well that a modest attempt was made in India in the year 1994-95. The then Union Finance Minister introduced a 5 per cent services tax on three services namely telephone services, non-life insurance services and services of stock brokers. Since then the number of services; the number of assessees and amount of revenue are all increasing consistently. This is clear from Tables 12.4 and 12.5.

Table 12.4: Amount of Revenue from GST

(Rs. Crore)

Year	Amount
1994-95	407
1995-96	862
1996-97	1059
1997-98	1586

(Contd.)

1998-99	1957
1999-00	2128
2000-01	3302
2001-02	4172
2002-03	7891
2004-05	14200
2005-06	23055
2006-07	38169
2007-08	51309
2008-09	65000 (RE)

Source: Budget Documents.

From Table 12.4 it is clear that since its introduction in 1994-95, there is a phenomenal increase in the revenue from GST. Almost, between the period 1994-95 and 2008-09, there is almost 150 times increase in revenue. This indeed augurs well for a new tax.

Table 12.5: Tax Revenue as a Per cent of GDP

Source/Type	2001-02	2003-04	2007-08	2008-09 (RE)
Tax Revenue (Net)	5.86	6.79	9.36	8.59
Non-tax revenue	2.97	2.79	2.18	1.77
Personal income tax	1.40	1.50	2.53	2.26
Corporation tax	1.61	2.31	4.11	4.09
Customs	1.77	1.77	2.22	1.99
Excise	3.18	3.30	2.63	2.00
Service tax	0.14	0.29	1.09	1.20
Others	0.10	0.08	0.05	0.04

Source: Budget Documents.

From Table 12.5 certain important observations can be made. Even though the services tax is relatively new, introduced only in the year 1994-95, it has succeeded in carving out a place for itself amongst major sources of revenue to the central government. In percentage terms, its revenue is continuously increasing. It is very likely that in the coming years, revenue from services tax would continue to fill in the government coffers.

Bibliography

Ahmad, Ehtisham and Nicholas Stern, *The Theory and Practice of Tax Reform in Developing Countries*, Foundation Books, 1991.

Ahuja, Astha, *Value Added Tax: Indian and Global Experiences,* New Century Publications, New Delhi.

American Institute of Certified Public Accountants, Inc., *Understanding Tax Reform: A Guide to 21st Century Alternatives*, New York, September, 2005.

Andrews, William D., "A Consumption Type or Cash Flow Personal Income Tax", *Harvard Law Review,* April, 1974.

Aronson, J. Richard, *Public Finance,* McGraw Hill, 1985.

Atkinson, A.B. and J.E. Stiglitz, *Lectures on Public Economics,* McGraw-Hill, 1980.

Auerbach, A.J., "The Theory of Excess Burden and Optimal Taxation" in A.J. Auerbach and M. Feldstein (eds.), *Hand Book of Public Economics*, Amsterdam: North Holland, 1985.

Bagchi, Amaresh (ed.), *Readings in Public Finance,* Oxford University Press, New Delhi, 2005.

Bailey, Stephen J., *Public Sector Economics: Theory Policy and Practice,* Palgrave, Second Edition, 2005.

——, *Strategic Public Finance*, Palgrave, 2004.

Botlhole, T.D. and T.J. Agiobenebo, "The Elasticity and Buoyancy of the Botswana Tax System and Their

Determinants", *The ICFAI Journal of Financial Economics,* Vol. IV, No. 4, December, 2006.

Bradford, David and Harvey, S. Rosen, *The Optimal Taxation of Commodities and Income,* OTA Papers, U.S. Department of Treasury, 1978.

Break, George F., "Incidence and Economic Effects of Taxation" in Alan S. Blinder, et al. (ed.), *The Economics of Public Finance*, The Brooking Institution, Washington D.C., 1974.

Chelliah, Raja, et al., "Introduction to Value Added Tax" in Amaresh Bagchi (ed.), *Readings in Public Finance,* Oxford University Press, New Delhi, 2005.

Chelliah, Raja J., "Case for An Expenditure Tax", *Economic and Political Weekly,* January 26, 1980.

Cullis, John and Philip Jones, *Public Finance and Public Choice*, Oxford University Press, 1998.

Dalton Hugh, *Principles of Public Finance,* Routledge and Kegan Paul, London, 1936.

Fisher, Irving, "Double Taxation of Savings", *American Economic Review*, Vol. 29, 1939.

——, *Constructive Income Taxation,* Harper Bros., New York, 1942.

Government of India, Ministry of Finance, *Report of the Task Force on Implementation of the Fiscal Responsibility and Budget Management Act 2003,* 2004 [Kelkar Committee Report].

Gupta, J.R., *Public Economics in India: Theory and Practice*, Atlantic Publishers & Distributors (P) Ltd., New Delhi, 2007.

Haig, R.M., *The Concept of Income*, Columbia University Press, 1921.

Halkandi, Sudhir, 'Goods and Services Tax: An Introductory Study', *Chartered Accountant*, April, 2007.

Hicks, Ursula, *Public Finance,* Pitman Publishing Corporation, New York, 1947. http://www.ctj.org.

James, Simon and Christopher Nobes, *The Economics of Taxation*, Philip Allan Publishers Limited, 1978.

Kaldor, Nicholas, *An Expenditure Tax,* George Allen and Unwin, London, 1955.

Krishnan, V.S., *Indirect Tax Reforms: Challenge and Response,* Abhinav Publications, New Delhi, 2006.

Kumar, Ramesh and Vibha Dua, "FBT: Environment in India: An Analysis", *Southern Economist,* January 1, 2007.

Mahler, Walter R., *Sales and Excise Taxation in India*, Orient Longman, New Delhi, 1970.

Musgrave, Richard A., *The Theory of Public Finance,* McGraw-Hill, 1959.

Musgrave, Richard A. and Peggy B. Musgrave, *Public Finance in Theory and Practice,* Fifth Edition, Tata McGraw-Hill, 2004.

Nanjegowda, H. and K. Narayana, "Integration of Service Tax with Valued Added Tax", *Southern Economist,* January 1, 2007.

Pechman, Joseph, *What Should Be Taxed: Income or Expenditure?* Brookings Institution, Washington D.C., 1980.

Peerzade, Sayed Afzal, *Expenditure Tax in India,* Anmol Publications, New Delhi, 1992.

——, "Towards a Fringe Benefits Tax", *Current Policy Issues* No. 2/89, National Institute of Public Finance and Policy, New Delhi, 1989.

——, "Fringe Benefits Expenditure Tax: The New Zealand Experience", *Asia-Pacific Taxation and Investment Bulletin,* Singapore, Vol. 8, No. 6, 1990.

——, "The Impact of Revenue of a Reduction in Tax Rates", *Asia-Pacific Taxation and Investment Bulletin*, Singapore, Vol. 8, No. 1, 1990.

——, "Proposal for A Modified Expenditure Tax", *Finance India,* New Delhi, Vol. 4, No. 3, 1990.

——, "Towards a Fringe Benefits Expenditure Tax", *Indian Journal of Economics,* Allahabad University, No. 283, 1991.

Pigou, A.C., *A Study in Public Finance*, Macmillan & Co., Ltd., London, 1951.

Purohit, Mahesh, *Value Added Tax*, Fourth Edition, Gayatri Publications, New Delhi, 2006.

Ramsey, Frank, "A Contribution to the Theory of Taxation", *Economic Journal*, Vol. 37, No. 145, 1927.

Rao, Kavita, "Goods and Services Tax for India", NIPFP, Working Paper 57, 2008.

Raul, R.K., "Value Added Tax: Does It Boost Corporate Sector?", *Southern Economist,* December 1-15, 2006.

Robson, Alex, *Taxation, Individual Incentives and Economic Growth*, Working Paper, School of Economics, Australian National University, Canberra, November, 2004.

Samuelson, P.A. and W.D. Nordhaus, *Economics*, 17th Edition, Tata McGraw-Hill Publishing Company Limited, New Delhi, 2002.

Seligman, Edwin R., *Progressive Taxation in Theory and Practice* 2nd Edition, Princeton University Press, Princeton, N.J., 1908.

Simons, Henry, *Personal Income Taxation,* Chicago University Press, 1938.

Stiglitz, Joseph E., "The Role of Government in Economic Development" in Amaresh Bagchi (ed.), *Readings in Public Finance,* Oxford University Press, New Delhi, 2005.

Sundharam, K.P.M. and K.K. Andley, *Public Finance: Theory and Practice,* S. Chand & Company, New Delhi, 2003.

Sury, M.M., *Fiscal Policy Developments in India: 1947 to 2007*, Indian Tax Foundation, New Delhi, 2007.

Tait, Alan A., *Value Added Tax*, McGraw-Hill Book Company, 1972.

The Meade Committee Report, Institute of Fiscal Studies, U.K., 1978.

The U.S. Treasury Report, Washington D.C., 1984.

www.bized.ac.uk/economy/virtuallibrary.

Zee, Howell H., "Taxation and Efficiency" in Amaresh Bagchi (ed.), *Readings in Public Finance*, Oxford University Press, New Delhi, 2005.